EDITOR: LEE JOHNSON

OSPREY MILITARY **MEN-AT-ARMS SERIES** 264

PETER THE GREAT'S ARMY 2: CAVALRY

Text by
ANGUS KONSTAM
Colour plates by
DAVID RICKMAN

First published in Great Britain in 1993 by
Osprey, an imprint of Reed Consumer Books Limited
Michelin House, 81 Fulham Road,
London SW3 6RB
and Auckland, Melbourne, Singapore and Toronto

ISBN 1 85532 3486

Filmset in Great Britain by Keyspools Ltd., Golborne,
Lancashire
Printed through Bookbuilders Ltd, Hong Kong

Artist's note

Readers may care to note that the original paintings
from which the colour plates in this book were
prepared are available for private sale. All
reproduction copyright whatsoever is retained by the
publisher. All enquiries should be addressed to:

David Rickman
238C Presidential Drive
Greenville
DE 19807
USA

The publishers regret that they can enter into no
correspondence upon this matter.

For a catalogue of all books published by Osprey Military
please write to:

**The Marketing Manager,
Consumer Catalogue Department,
Osprey Publishing Ltd,
Michelin House, 81 Fulham Road,
London SW3 6RB**

INTRODUCTION

The first volume of this study—MAA 260, *Peter the Great's Army: 1*—covered the infantry element of Tsar Peter I's army. This volume primarily discusses the cavalry, both the regular troops and irregular forces such as the Cossacks, their composition and effectiveness. It considers how Western military ideas fused with Russian practical requirements to create a cavalry force that compromised between tactical and operational needs, though not always with success. The book also outlines the development of the Russian train of artillery, which proved so decisive at the battle of Poltava, and was employed in several sieges during the Great Northern War. This period saw the establishment of the artillery train as the premier element of the Russian army, a status it maintained until 1917.

The administrative zeal of Tsar Peter was such that his army was welded into a surprisingly effective military machine for its time. This was achieved by full support from an economy and administrative system which, like those of Frederick the Great's Prussia, existed primarily to maintain the armed forces. The development of the Petrine military administration, and its attendant cost and logistical problems, are discussed below. By the time of his death in 1725 Peter the Great had placed Russia among the foremost European powers, and had created a military system that has influenced the European balance of power until the present day.

CHRONOLOGY

From Poltava to the death of Peter the Great
(The period 1700–1709 is covered in MAA 260 Peter the Great's Army: 1)

1709

28 June	*Battle of Poltava:* Swedes under Charles XII are decisively defeated by Peter the Great. Charles XII escapes to Turkey.
Aug.	Elector Augustus of Saxony (King Augustus II of Poland) repudiates peace

An Eastern European horseman, probably typical of the Russian provincial noble cavalry, being ridden down by Charles XII of Sweden at the catastrophic Russian defeat at Narva (20 November 1700). He is depicted armed with a sabre of Polish-Hungarian form, another of which lies on the ground behind him. The archaic fluted lance is an anachronism, though such lances were used to carry standards even at this date. Detail of an engraving by G.F. Rugendas, early 18th century. (State Historic Museum, Moscow)

	treaty with Sweden. Saxon army enters Poland.
Oct.	Menshikov enters Poland with 20,000 Russians.
9 Oct.	Tsar Peter and Augustus II re-establish anti-Swedish alliance.
Nov.	Danes repudiate peace treaty with Sweden. 16,000 Danes cross into Scania (S. Sweden) and besiege Malmö.
13 Nov.	Sheremetiev invades Livonia and besieges Riga. The siege continues throughout the winter.
18 Dec.	Poltava victory parade: 17,000 Swedish prisoners are marched through Moscow.

1710

Feb.	Stenbock gathers 14,000 Swedes in Scania and launches campaign against Danes.
28 Feb.	*Battle of Helsingfors:* Stenbock's army defeats 11,000 Danes under Rantzau. Danes evacuate Sweden.
March	General-Admiral Apraxin besieges Vyborg with 18,000 Russians.
13 June	Vyborg surrenders to Apraxin.
10 July	Riga surrenders to Sheremetiev. Livonia annexed by Russia.
Oct.	Reval surrenders to Sheremetiev. Estonia annexed by Russia.
21 Nov.	Ottoman Turks declare war on Russia.

1711

April	Moldavian Christians sign treaty with Russia and rise against the Turks.
June	Russian army enters Moldavia.
7 July	*Battle of the Pruth:* Turkish army of 200,000 surrounds the Russian army, and commences a bombardment of their positions.
12 July	Treaty of the Pruth signed. Russian army allowed to escape in return for the surrender of Azov and Taganrog.
Aug.	Menshikov with Russian army enters Swedish Pomerania and besieges Stral-

	sund and Wismar (abandoned in October).

1712

May	Stenbock lands in Pomerania with 18,000 men.
July	Danish army besieges Swedish-controlled Bremen and Verden.
Sept.	Stenbock invades Mecklenburg and occupies Rostock.
19 Nov.	Turkey again declares war on Russia. Russo-Saxon army led by Menshikov pursues Stenbock's Swedes.
20 Dec.	*Battle of Gadebusch:* Stenbock's 15,000 Swedes inflict a decisive defeat on King Frederick IV's 12,000 Danes.

1713

Jan.	Stenbock trapped in Danish town of Tönning by Tsar Peter with 36,000 Allies.
24 April	Apraxin and Tsar Peter launch galley fleet on an amphibious offensive along the Finnish coast.

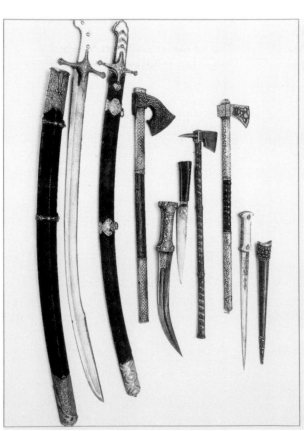

Muscovite cavalry weapons of the late 17th century. These sabres, axes and daggers represent the weapon types carried by pre-Petrine provincial and metropolitan noble cavalry. All weapons are steel, with gold and silver decoration. (State Museum of the Moscow Kremlin)

12 May	Helsingfors (Helsinki) captured, followed by Borgå.
16 May	Stenbock surrenders to Allies (12,000 prisoners).
24 June	Treaty of Adrianople brings peace between Russia and Turkey.
July	Menshikov besieges Stettin with Russian army.
19 Sept.	Stettin surrenders, and is given to Prussia.

1714

June	Russian galley fleet cruises off Finnish coast. Swedish fleet sent to block their progress.
4 Aug.	*Battle of Hango:* Russian galley fleet successfully attacks part of the becalmed Swedish fleet. Russia's first naval victory secures the Finnish conquests.
Sept.	Apraxin captures Åland Islands, patrols the Finnish coast and burns the north Swedish town of Umeå.
20 Sept.	Charles XII leaves Turkey.
Oct.	Hanover annexes Bremen and Verden.

1715

March	Prussia declares war on Sweden.
July	Allied forces besiege Stralsund.
Oct.	Prussian army entrenches on Rügen, blocking naval supply route to Stralsund.
24 Oct.	Hanover (but not England) declares war on Sweden.
4 Nov.	Battle of Rügen. Charles XII with 6,000 Swedes assaults 17,000 Prussians in entrenchments. Swedish attack repulsed.
12 Dec.	Charles XII escapes to Sweden.
13 Dec.	Stralsund surrenders (6,000 prisoners).

1716

23 Feb.	Charles XII invades Norway (Danish possession).
March	Wismar besieged by Russians and Prussians.
10 March	Charles XII captures Kristiana (modern Oslo).
8 April	Wismar, last Swedish foothold south of the Baltic, surrenders.
Mid April	Supply problems force Charles to retreat.

Watercolour cartoon of a Petrine Dragoon officer, wearing the post-1720 Dragoon uniform and an officer's sash. The ceremonial horse furnishings are of a traditional Russian style, not reflective of those used on active service. (The Lenin Library, Moscow)

May	Large Allied invasion force gathers in Denmark.
June	English fleet under Admiral Norris joins Allied invasion fleet.
21 Sept.	Tsar Peter postpones invasion due to dissension in Allied camp. 70,000-man invasion force disperses into winter quarters.

1717

June	Neutral English fleet in Baltic deters both sides from major action.

1718

30 Oct.	Charles XII of Sweden invades southern Norway.
30 Nov.	Charles XII is killed by a bullet from an artillery canister round. Swedish army returns home. Frederik I is crowned King of Sweden.

1719

March · King George I of England launches diplomatic campaign to prevent further Russian expansion in Baltic.

May · Apraxin gathers 50,000 men and galley fleet in Finland.

Aug. · Apraxin raids Swedish coast, burning towns and villages. Cossacks ride within sight of Stockholm.

14 Aug. · Naval assault on Stockholm repulsed, as is another seven days later.

19 Oct. · Armistice between Denmark and Sweden.

20 Nov. · Peace treaty between Hanover and Sweden. Hanover retains Bremen and Verden. Britain promises naval support for the Swedes.

27 Dec. · Peace treaty between Saxony, Poland and Sweden.

1720

21 Jan. · Peace treaty between Prussia and Sweden. Prussia retains Stettin.

June · British fleet blockades Reval. Apraxin's galley fleet escapes to Finland.

3 July · Peace treaty between Denmark and Sweden.

Aug. · Galley fleet continue raids on Swedish mainland, burning towns up to 30 miles inland.

Oct. · English withdraw support for Sweden.

1721

10 Sept. · *Treaty of Nystadt* ends Great Northern War. Russia retains Baltic States, Eastern Finland and Ingria.

15 Sept. · Tsar Peter brings the news of peace to St. Petersburg. Celebrations last for several weeks.

22 Oct. · Tsar Peter receives the title 'the Great' and 'Emperor of Russia'.

1722

3 May · Collapse of power in Persia seen by Peter as opportunity for expansion.

18 July · Peter embarks army at Astrakhan on Caspian Sea flotilla.

3 Aug. · Amphibious landing north of Derbent.

23 Aug. · Russian army enters Derbent.

12 Sept. · Peace treaty between Russia and the Shah of Persia. Russia retains provinces of Georgia and Daghestan. Peter wants more territory.

Nov. · Amphibious assault on Rasht (south of Caspian Sea).

1723

July · Russians capture Baku and annex Azerbaijan.

1725

28 Jan. · Death of Tsar Peter the Great.

THE CAVALRY BEFORE PETER

The army inherited by Tsar Peter was already heavily influenced by Western military practice. Army lists of 1681 outline an army strength of 164,000 men, of whom 89,000 were organised into formations of a foreign pattern. Little numerical information is available on the non-Cossack cavalry element, though 8,000 such horsemen are known to have participated in Prince Vasili Golytsyn's Crimean campaign of 1689: these were the mounted provincial and metropolitan nobility, organised 'in the Russian manner'. The proportion of cavalry to infantry was much smaller than in Western armies of the time. Golytsyn's army suffered a major defeat at the hands of the Crimean Tatars, which indicates that the noble cavalrymen were not reliable military material, and were at best unversed in the traditional roles of cavalry when protecting an army in enemy territory.

These troops formed the major proportion of Tsar Peter's cavalry when he raised his new army over the winter of 1699–1700. During the Narva campaign the 10,000 noble cavalrymen were mustered from the districts of Moscow, Smolensk and Novgorod. Weber, a resident of Brunswick who lived in Russia, describes them as a 'sorry multitude', an observation confirmed in general contemporary opinion.

These cavalry formations were composed of *stolniki* and *stryapchie* (minor noblemen) and their militia. Senior Muscovite noblemen, some of *boyar* rank, commanded contingents of mounted noblemen. Pre-Petrine Muscovite rank was given as 'the reward for wounds, loss of blood or of having been a prisoner; it was also given to those whose fathers or other relatives had died in battle or on campaign' (Klyuchevsky 1958). Military losses and easily obtained ennoblement created the opportunity to swell the Muscovite ranks with new *stolniki* and *stryapchie*, turning the Muscovite nobility into a large corps: 6,835 in 1681 and 11,533 in 1700. These were eligible for service as cavalrymen when ordered by the Tsar, and on campaign would be accompanied by armed serfs, or had their places taken by paid replacements from their estates. The nobility of Moscow were seen as the élite corps of the army, superior to the provincial nobility, who in turn were organised into two regional divisions, those of Smolensk and Novgorod.

At Narva (1700) these noble cavalrymen, commanded by Sheremetiev, were seized with panic before they even engaged the Swedes, and fled the field (see Plate A). During the post-Narva reforms the noble cavalry regiments saw little further active service apart from a force sent with Repnin to assist the Poles in 1701. The formations were gradually disbanded to form the cadre of the new dragoon regiments.

DRAGOONS

On 8 November 1699 Tsar Peter ordered the creation of a new army organised on Western lines, raised by a combination of voluntary recruitment and mass conscription. At the end of January 1700, these new troops mustered at Preobrazhenskoi near Moscow, and a number were designated to form two new Dragoon regiments. Their ranks were stiffened by a draft of more experienced cavalrymen drawn from existing units. The organisation and training of the two regiments were placed in the hands of two foreigners, Col. Joachim Goltz and Col. Schnewentz, who gave the regiments their names. Both colonels were Saxons, as were the majority of their officers.

The regiments mustered 998 and 800 officers and men respectively.

Before the two regiments had been given anything but the most rudimentary training, they left for Moscow in August 1700 and took part in the Narva campaign. Their performance was unimpressive, both formations being routed ignominiously at the battle of Narva. The survivors were reassembled at Novgorod, where drafts of recruits replaced campaign losses.

The Narva campaign demonstrated that the older, traditional cavalry units were of little practical use in combat; and that the two new Dragoon regiments were insufficient to provide all the scouting and foraging needs of the army. Accordingly, Prince Boris Alexevich Golytsyn, governor of Kazan and Astrakhan, was ordered to supervise the raising of ten new Dragoon regiments in Moscow. This was done rapidly, and these regiments joined the main army commanded by Sheremetiev at Pskov by the spring of 1701. Two further Dragoon regiments were formed in Novgorod, and these were also sent to join Sheremetiev. The entire arm of 14 regiments participated in Sheremetiev's Livonian campaigns of

Dragoon Fuzeler (trooper), c. 1700–20. He is equipped with an unusual shortened musket with a serpentine trigger. Note the gun shoe, secured to a strap projecting from beneath the saddle. (Engraving from Viskovatov, Opisaniye ... Rossiskoi Imperatorskoi Armii, St. Petersburg 1844–56)

1701–2, though their success in the battles of Erestfer and Hummelsdorf was due more to superior numbers than to training or troop quality.

A further three Dragoon regiments were formed during 1702–3, followed by three more in 1705. This process of forming new Dragoon regiments continued in the period from 1706–8, and minor successes such as Prince Menshikov's victory at Kalisz (1706) gave the raw troops a modicum of experience in combat. By the time Charles XII invaded Russia Peter's army contained 37 Dragoon regiments, including three of Horse Grenadiers.

Quality and Training

When the initial Dragoon regiments were raised the majority of the officers were Saxons, supplemented by a number of Russian nobles. Subsequent regiments continued to use foreign officers, but as time passed increasing numbers of native Russians were trained up in the existing regiments and began to obtain full officer rank. By Peter's death in 1725 the majority of the officer posts in the army were held by Russians.

The speed with which the initial regiments were raised meant that often the foreign officers appointed were of poor quality. Charles Whitworth, the English Ambassador at Peter's Court, reported in 1707 that

'They are unskilled in the general motions of an army . . . their great want is for good officers, whereof they have very few'. He also commented on quantity as well as quality: 'The Tsar's affairs are likely to be ruined for the want of capable officers, few regiments . . . having above two captains and three lieutenants.'

His opinion of the Dragoon regiments was equally uncomplimentary: 'It is not thought that they will be able to make head in a set battle with the Swedish cuirassiers, who have a great advantage by their horses and armour.' The Russian dragoons, he said, have 'ill horses and the army not three able generals'. Francis Weber's observations mirrored Whitworth's. He wrote at some length on the poor state of the Russian army in 1701:

'A great number are called to serve and if they are examined closely the only result is the feeling of shame . . . For every foreigner killed there are three, four or even more Russians killed. As for the cavalry, we are ashamed to look at them ourselves, let alone show them to a foreigner. [They consist of] sickly, ancient horses, blunt sabres, puny, badly dressed men who do not know how to wield their weapons. There are some noblemen who do not know how to charge an arquebus, let alone hit their target. They care nothing about killing their enemy, but think only how to return to their homes. They prey that God will send them a light wound so as not to suffer much, for which they will recieve a reward from the sovereign. In battle they hide in thickets; whole companies take cover in a forest or a valley, and I have even heard noblemen say prey God we may serve our sovereign without drawing our swords from our scabbards.'

The period between Narva and Poltava was used to train, motivate and harden these troops, inspiring them not to fight in 'the interests of His Tsarish Majesty' but in 'the interests of the Russian state'. However, the improvement achieved in the quality of manpower was not matched by a corresponding improvement in horseflesh. Captain Jefferyes, who served with the Swedes, reported that during the pursuit of the Russian horse after the battle of

Officer of a Dragoon regiment, c. 1700–20. His regulation uniform of the early pattern is worn completely unmodified, without a sash. The buff leather gauntlets are slit at the sides to allow them to be worn over the uniform cuffs. (Engraving from Viskovatov)

Prince Alexander Danilovich Menshikov (1673–1729). Field Marshal of Cavalry from 1709, he remained Peter's favourite despite frequent corruption charges. He is depicted (incorrectly wearing armour) during his victory at the battle of Kalisz (19 October 1706). Engraving by Picart. (The Lenin Library, Moscow)

Holowczyn (1708): ''twas seldom we could overtake them, and never but when by chance they came into a morasse, whence their horses being little and weak could not so hastily carry them out as to escape us'.

Jefferyes attested to the improvements in the quality of Tsar Peter's army: 'The Svedes must now own the Muscovites have learnt their lesson much better than they had either at the battles of Narva or Fraistadt; and that they equall if not exceed the Saxon both in discipline and valour, tis true their cavalry are not able to cope with owrs.'

Dragoon organisation

When the original two Dragoon regiments (Goltz's and Schnewentz's) were raised in 1700 they were formed into ten companies of 80–100 men each. Each company consisted of a captain, a lieutenant, an ensign, eight NCOs, and two musicians, the remainder being troopers. In the field a full-strength regiment operated in five squadrons, each of two companies. Each squadron was commanded by a regimental officer or a senior captain (the majority of whom were Germans).

A new establishment was introduced on 12 October 1704, founded on the ideas of Field Marshal Ogilvy, a Scot in Russian service; many of his reforms were founded on experience gained during the campaigns of 1700–4. Each of the 20 existing Dragoon regiments was to be reorganised into 12 companies, each containing between 90 and 100 officers and men. Regimental officers, supply staff, artisans and servants would bring the total establishment to 1,230 men. These would be divided into four squadrons, each containing three companies. In practice it appears that these paper strengths were never attained, and the ten-company organisation was retained for all existing regiments. Regiments formed after the introduction of the new establishment were organised into 12 companies.

In 1705, a Horse Grenadier company of 100 officers and men was added to the establishment of each regiment, formed from Line Dragoons selected by the regimental commander. These were almost immediately concentrated into *ad hoc* Horse Grenadier regiments, a siphoning-off of experienced troops which would not have escaped the attention of the selecting officers. Over the winter of 1708–9 these *ad hoc* formations were transformed into three permanent Horse Grenadier regiments (Kropotov's, Von der Ropp's, and Roshnov's). These consisted of 10–12 companies, each regiment named after its colonel.

A decree of 10 March 1708 stated that henceforth all Line Dragoon and infantry regiments would be named after provinces or towns, rather than the name of their colonel.

A carefully considered programme of army reforms were introduced by an *ukas* of 19 February 1712, in which the establishment of a Dragoon regiment was set at 1,328 men, reverting to a ten-company organisation. The regimental allocation of horses was 1,100. A complete regiment consisted of:

1 colonel	11 drummers
2 senior officers	2 trumpeters
22 junior officers	900 Dragoon troopers
10 ensigns	94 servants
40 sergeants and senior NCOs	31 artisans
60 corporals	100 drivers
1 kettle-drummer	34 non-combatants

This establishment was reduced slightly in 1720 to a new peacetime level of 35 officers, 1,162 men and 54 servants, an organisation that continued until after Tsar Peter's death in 1725.

All establishment strengths were, of course, only ideals: on campaign losses through sickness, desertion, straggling and battle reduced these totals considerably. The allocation of replacements was haphazard, many of them deserting or dying before they ever reached their regiments. Entries in Tsar Peter's journal of the troops engaged at the battle of Lesnaya (1708) record the average strength of a Dragoon regiment as between 500 and 650 men, less than half the full establishment. These figures are probably exceptional, given the gruelling nature of the 1708 campaign. Although new drafts of troops reached the army during the winter of 1708–9, campaign losses and the lack of suitable remounts kept the Dragoon regiments well below establishment strength. Although no detailed returns are

Table A: Dragoon Regiments

Raised in 1700:
1. Joachim Goltz's (Moskovski)
2. Col. Schnewenz's (Kievski)

Raised in 1701 (in Moscow):
3. Col. Zhdanov's (Vladimirski)
4. Col. Novikov's (Pskovski)
5. Mikhail Sybin's (Kazanski)
6. Prince Meschterski's (Novgorodski)
7. Seemeon Kropotov's (Troitski)
8. Prince Lvov's (Astrakhanski)
9. Alexander Volina's (Sibirienski)
10. Anastassi Ostafiev's (Smolenski, disbanded 1712)
11. Col. Poluektov's (St. Petersburgski, disbanded 1712)
12. Col. Dumont's (Tschernigovski, disbanded 1712)

Raised in 1701 (in Novgorod):
13. Denis Deugerin's (Viatski)
14. Col. Morelli's (Nizhegorodski)

Raised in 1702:
15. Prince Nikita Volkonski's (Yaroslavski)
16. Grigori Suchotin's (Tverskoy)
17. Ivan Gorbov's (Permski)

Raised in 1704:
18. Ingermanlandski (Ingermanlandski)
19. Col. Portes' (Nevski)
20. General Apraxin's (Belozerski)

Raised in 1705:
21. Niklaus Hering's (Ryazanski)
22. Prince Roman Volkonski's (Ustiuzhski)
23. Count Sheremetiev's (Arkhangelski)
24. Col. Putiatin's (Luzhski)
25. Col. Monastirev's (Vologodski)
26. Col. Pesstov's (Narvski)

Raised in 1706:
27. Col. Streshnev's (Rostovski)
28. Col. Pavlov's (Azovski)
29. Col. Fassman's (Yamburgski, disbanded 1712)

Raised in 1707:
30. Col. Geshov's (Life Regiment)
31. Col. Mursenkov's (Olonetzski)
32. Kargopolski (Kargopolski)

Raised in 1708:
33. Col. Araktscheiev's (Tobolski)
34. Kropotovski (Kropotovski, from 1712 renamed Novotroitski)

Note: The numbers are for identification purposes only: no regimental numbers were used in the Petrine army. Regiments were known by the name of their colonel until March 1708, when they received the provincial names shown in brackets.

available it can be estimated that the average strength of a Dragoon regiment at the battle of Poltava (1709) was around 800 men.

Tsar Peter I at the battle of Lesnaya (28 September 1708). The wooded nature of the battlefield is shown, although the background has been depicted as open rather than a mixture of woods and scrub. Painting by Martin the Younger, early 18th century. (The State Artillery Museum, St. Petersburg)

Tactics and employment

At the end of the 17th century the mounted arm of most Western armies contained roughly equal proportions of dragoons and conventional cavalry. When Tsar Peter reformed his army, he chose to ignore this balance: he opted for an equestrian arm composed almost exclusively of dragoons, which he saw as the best solution to the problems of large distances and poor terrain that faced his army in Russia and Poland. The lack of suitable horses capable of enduring both heavy loads and long marches also precluded the formation of true cavalry regiments. Dragoons were becoming one of the most useful troop types in early 18th century armies: they could scout ahead of the army, protect its flanks when on the march and gather provisions. Peter's Dragoons were also invaluable for harassing the enemy and for implementing the Tsar's 'scorched earth' policy.

Tsar Peter formed his Dragoon regiments into larger *ad hoc* formations. During the invasion by the Swedes in 1708–9, one such *korvolan* (from *corps-volant* or 'flying corps') of 11 regiments was formed under Prince Menshikov, and another of 12 regiments under Prince Golytsyn. These formations were the main harriers of Swedish columns, providing a more reliable alternative to Cossack units. By attacking stray units, such as the two Swedish Dragoon regiments mauled near Starodub (1708), and by denying supplies to the enemy, it was hoped to wear down the advancing Swedish army. The Dragoon regiments could thus harass an enemy who was attempting to conserve his own cavalry for use in any forthcoming battle.

A certain amount of tactical information may be gleaned from contemporary sources, the best being Prince Menshikov's *Dragunskogo Artykul* (St. Petersburg 1720). When in action, dismounted dragoons formed a four-man deep firing line, resembling that used by the infantry. This was the early 17th century manner of using dragoons, which by this time had mostly been replaced in the West by deploying dismounted dragoons as skirmishers. One dragoon in six was detailed as a horse-holder. At Lesnaya (1708) the protection of the forest edge, combined with firepower, proved sufficient to prevent the Swedish horse from charging home.

When fighting mounted, Russian dragoons deployed in three ranks with a frontage of four or five companies. Advancing at a trot, they discharged their firearms (full-length weapons rather than pistols) at approximately 30 paces from the enemy body. The firearms were then dropped to suspend from their slings, and the dragoons drew their swords or pistols. The advance would then continue at the trot. In defence the same procedure was adopted, the troopers advancing upon the charging enemy. This practice carried the risk of disordering the formation when the firearms were discharged, and effectiveness was limited since only the front rank was able to fire. Only superbly trained cavalry could maintain a charge at more than a trot with any cohesion, so the Russian dragoons' reliance on firepower was perhaps the only sensible recourse. Captain Jefferyes wrote at the battle of Holowczyn (1708) that the Russian dragoons: 'Never, during the whole action engag'd so closely hand to fist with the Svedes, but discharg'd commonly their guns at 30 or 40 paces distance, then runn, charg'd again, rallied and so discharg'd' (Hatton, 1954).

Charles XII of Sweden had adopted cavalry tactics based on dense formations of horsemen charging knee tucked behind knee in chevron-shaped formations. The aggressive ('gå på') doctrine of the Swedish horse was almost unique in European warfare of the period. The Russians hoped that dragoon firepower aimed at the apex of Swedish cavalry chevrons would cause enough disruption to break the momentum of Swedish charges, allowing the Russians to fight on more advantageous terms. However, with the impetus of Swedish charges and the experience of Swedish cavalrymen, no Russian tactic could ever prove adequate. Petrine dragoons lacked the training and the horseflesh to match the Swedish cavalry face to face, though after Poltava Russian dragoons were undoubtedly some of the most experienced troops of their kind in Europe. Their reliance on firepower was further emphasised in experiments with horse artillery, designed to support dragoons with canister fire. These were unsuccessful and technical problems led to these small howitzers being withdrawn in 1709, probably soon after the battle of Poltava.

The Swedish chevron formation encouraged a tactic known as 'threading'. As dragoons facing the apex of the charge shied away, the formations of horse 'threaded' through each other's formations, emerging behind each other. Reserve squadrons could then attack the (by now disordered) attacking formations with a reasonable chance of success. However, in these circumstances the nerves of both horse and rider were of the greatest importance; given the training and relative inexperience of Russian dragoons, it was more likely that, faced with a charging Swedish chevron, the defenders would break before contact.

Tsar Peter I accompanied by Russian Dragoons at Poltava. Both the Dragoon officer shown cutting down a Swede, and the Tsar himself, ride horses with unmodified furniture. Drawing by Martin the Younger, early 18th century. (State Historic Museum, Moscow)

At Poltava Menshikov's Dragoon regiments were sited among and behind a line of redoubts. These constrained the manoeuvrability of the Swedish horse, and the limited frontage forced them to charge by squadrons, subjected to a crossfire from the redoubts. Initial success in disordering and repelling the Swedish horse allowed Menshikov to pull his cavalry back in at least some semblance of order.

Dragoons proved invaluable after a battle, covering a retreat or pursuing a broken enemy. A flying corps (*korvolan*) was formed by Menshikov after Poltava, consisting of dragoons, the remaining batteries of horse artillery and Guardsmen of the Semenovski Regiment mounted on horses (sometimes two to a horse). This corps pursued the remnants of the Swedish army, eventually forcing their surrender at Perovolochna on the Dniepr. The mounting of Guardsmen repeated an improvisation employed by the *korvolan* which fought at Lesnaya (1708).

Dragoon uniforms

When Tsar Peter formed his two new Dragoon regiments in the winter of 1699–1700, the troopers were dressed in uniforms cut 'in the German fashion' (the Russians habitually denoting anything from Western Europe as 'German'). Russian dragoons therefore resembled their contemporaries in Western armies. (The noble metropolitan and provincial cavalry formations retained their Russian dress, as did the irregular cavalry.)

As with the infantry regiments, the uniform colour was chosen by the regimental commander, a decision based primarily on the availability and cost of cloth. The cut of the uniform was standard for the whole army, so both infantry and dragoons shared the same basic uniform. A detailed description of the 1700–20 pattern uniform is given in *Peter the Great's Army: 1*.

One area in which dragoon uniform differed was footwear. Each dragoon was issued with a pair of heavy, black, square-toed riding boots (*botforti*) in the current Western style, which could be worn turned down at the knee when dismounted. Their comfort was improved by over-socks of white wool, which reached to immediately above the knee; these were secured by black leather garters.

The colours of neckcloths (*galstuki*) and great-

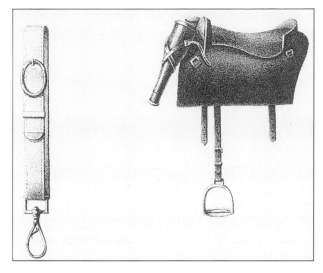

Petrine dragoon saddle and carbine sling, 1700–25. The sling or 'bandolier' was worn over the left shoulder with the buckle (for adjusting the length) usually to the back; the sprung hook at the base was clipped to a rail on the side of the carbine. Note also the method of attachment of the pistol holster on the left side of the saddle. (Engraving from Viskovatov)

coats (*shineli*) appear to have varied more widely than was the case in infantry regiments, red being common for both items. Again, the colonel would choose the colour worn by his regiment. Buff leather gloves (*perchatki*) were usually worn when mounted, although these would hinder the operation of firearms.

Headgear varied in a similar way to infantry regiments, some units wearing a black tricorne hat (*treugolka*), while other regiments favoured a cloth bonnet (*kartuz*) sometimes trimmed in the regimental fashion. Horse Grenadiers wore a mitre (*grenaderskaya tshapka*) identical to that of Grenadiers of infantry.

No field identification signs were worn as far as is known, so that the profusion of different uniform colours combined with the dust and smoke of battle could lead to confusion: 'A troop of (Swedish) Life Dragoons clashed repeatedly with the Russians. When the troop reformed again, they made an astonishing discovery. Six Russian horsemen had neatly slotted into the Swedish squadron, strictly according to regulation: two in the forward line and four in the rear' (Englund, 1992).

Uniform colours were standardised following the introduction of the new uniform patterns in 1720. All

Line dragoons now wore a blue *kaftan* of the new cut with a white falling collar and red cuffs, turnbacks and button-hole linings. A light brown vest (*kamzol*) was worn beneath the coat. Breeches were in the same brown colour, pulled over blue woollen stockings. A red neckcloth and a red greatcoat completed the issue. Uniform colours (where known) are summarised in Table B.

Dragoon firearms

While Tsar Peter's Dragoons relied heavily on firepower, surprisingly little attention appears to have been paid to the standardisation of their firearms. Before Peter's reign, and for the majority of the war years, no regulation pattern of long firearm existed in the Russian army. Pre-Petrine cavalry

Table B: Dragoon regiment uniform colours, 1709

Regiment	Headgear	Coat	Facings	Breeches	Vest	Overcoat
1 Moskovski	Tricorne	White	White	Brown	Brown	Red
2 Kievski	—	—	—	—	—	—
3 Vladimirski	Red kartuz	Green	Red	Brown	—	Blue
4 Pskovski	Tricorne	Blue	Red	Brown	Brown	Red
5 Kazanski	—	—	—	—	—	—
6 Novgorodski	White kartuz faced green	Green	Green	Brown	Brown	—
7 Troitski	—	—	—	—	—	—
8 Astrakhanski	Tricorne	Blue	White	Brown	Brown	—
9 Sibirienski	—	—	—	—	—	—
10 Smolenski	White kartuz faced red	White	Blue	Brown	Brown	—
11 St. Petersburgski	Tricorne	Green	Red	Red	Red	—
12 Tschernigovski	Tricorne	Red	Blue	Brown	Brown	—
13 Viatski	—	—	—	—	—	—
14 Nizhegorodski	—	—	—	—	—	—
15 Yaroslavski	Tricorne	Blue	Red	Brown	Green	—
16 Tverskoy	Blue kartuz faced red	Red	Blue	Brown	—	Red
17 Permski	—	—	—	—	—	—
18 Ingermanlandski	Tricorne	Green	Red	Brown	Green	Green
19 Nevski	—	—	—	—	—	—
20 Belozerski	Blue kartuz	Green	Red	Brown	—	Red
21 Ryazanski	Tricorne	Green	—	Brown	Brown	—
22 Ustiuzhski	Tricorne	Green	Red	Brown	Brown	Green
23 Arkhangelski	—	—	—	—	—	—
24 Luzhski	Blue kartuz	Green	—	Brown	Brown	Red
25 Vologdski	—	—	—	—	—	—
26 Narvski	Tricorne	Dk. Grey	—	Brown	Brown	Red
27 Rostovski	Tricorne	Green	Red	Brown	Green	Blue
28 Azovski	Tricorne	Blue	—	Brown	Brown	—
29 Yamburgski	—	—	—	—	—	—
30 Life Dragoons	Tricorne	Green	Red	Brown	Red	—
31 Olonetzski	—	—	—	—	—	—
32 Kargopolski	Tricorne	Green	Red	Brown	Red	—
33 Tobolski	Green kartuz faced red	Green	Blue	Brown	Brown	—
34 Kropotovski	—	—	—	—	—	—

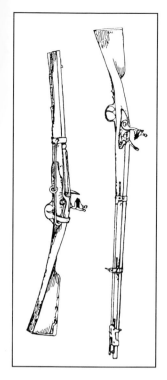

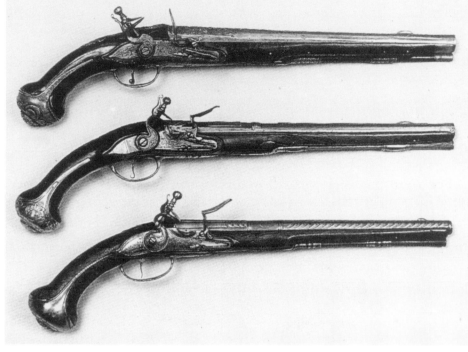

▲ *Petrine carbine and shortened dragoon musket. Both use the 'French-lock' flintlock system. Note the slinging rail with loose ring on the left side of the carbine; a similar rail would be fitted on the shortened musket. (Drawings based on weapons in the collection of the State Historic Museum, Moscow)*

▶ *Military flintlock pistols, early 18th century. High-quality decorated pistols like these were seldom the work of Russian gunsmiths. The top two weapons were produced in Holland and the lower in France, all three are typical of those imported to Russia for the use of officers during Peter's reign. (State Museums of the Moscow Kremlin)*

when carrying firearms favoured a snaphaunce 'Baltic lock' carbine, surviving examples of which display a high level of inlay work and other decoration. Peter's Dragoon regiments were initially equipped with a variety of imported flintlock firearms supplementing older Russian pieces. These imported weapons were purchased by Russian agents in Western Europe, mainly Holland and England, and shipped to Russia mostly via Arkhangelsk.

Initially, **muskets** were provided for use by dragoons—slightly shortened versions of those supplied to the infantry. Although these were exclusively imported during the period after Narva, an increasing number were manufactured in Russia. The main gunmaking centres at the time were St. Petersburg,

Moscow, Tula and Olonetz. These weapons averaged 130 cm overall, and fired an 18 mm ball. They had steel barrels and iron fittings, including an iron slinging rail on their left side. Early dragoon muskets had 'dog-lock' mechanisms, but the more reliable 'French-locks' (i.e. standard flintlock actions of the French pattern) began to replace them from 1706 onwards, and these formed the majority of firearm types produced in Russian workshops. These flintlock variants copied the form employed by French gunsmiths in the late 17th and early 18th century, the 'golden age' of French gunmaking. 'French-locks' were seen as the most advanced of their time, the reliability of action enhanced by the provision of 'cocked' and 'half-cocked' positions for the cock.

From about 1708, these shortened flintlock dragoon muskets were slowly but steadily replaced by Russian-made **flintlock carbines**, copied from examples imported from Western Europe. These carbines were shorter and lighter than the dragoon muskets, surviving examples in the Kremlin Armoury having an average overall length of 106 cm, with a 70 cm smoothbore steel barrel, taking a ball of 14–18 mm.

In addition, a number of **rifled carbines** were issued to sharpshooters in each Dragoon regiment.

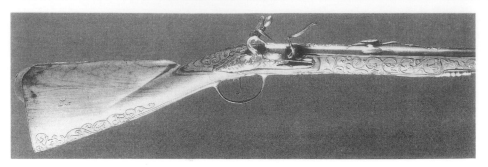

A shortened rifled musket c.1709. A number of these decorated weapons were carried by Dragoon officers on campaign, although their primary use was as hunting pieces. This particular weapon was manufactured at Tula. (State Museums of the Moscow Kremlin)

These were otherwise identical to the standard carbines apart from being fitted with a backsight and foresight, and a patch box in the stock for accessories, such as the patches for rifled shot. Rifled carbines also tended to be modestly decorated with wood carving, distinguishing them from the normal range of smoothbore carbines. Officers were reported to have carried personal rifled sporting weapons on occasion. At Poltava (1709) a number of Russian dragoons were used as marksmen, presumably those equipped with rifled weapons (Englund 1992).

A final type of firearm occasionally issued to dragoons was the **musketoon**: a large-calibre smoothbore flintlock weapon, designed to deliver one or more balls with little accuracy but devastating effect. Produced in both St. Petersburg and Olonetz to fairly tight specifications laid down by the army, the musketoon appears from surviving examples to have had a standard bore of 28 mm. Their use by dragoons was limited by their weight and the awkwardness of the reloading process. No sights were fitted to these weapons; they were capable of firing up to ten musket balls per discharge, which would spread slightly upon leaving the barrel. Ordinary dragoon muskets and carbines were also capable of being double- or even treble-shotted, although this increased the risk of the gun bursting.

Each cavalryman was armed with a single **pistol** carried in a holster on the left side of the saddle. During the late 17th century Russian cavalry used wheel-lock pistols, requiring a spanner to ready them for use. Although undecorated examples can be found, many appear to have some degree of inlay in the Russian style, and most bear the marks of Moscow gunsmiths. Although cavalry pistols were produced in Tula and Sestroryetsk during the latter years of Tsar Peter's reign, the vast majority used in the army were actually of foreign manufacture,

Russian gunsmiths concentrating on the production of long firearms. The majority of imported pistols were produced by the gunsmiths of Amsterdam, Maastricht and Utrecht. Locks were of the 'French' type, with calibres ranging from 11 mm to 19 mm. The first regulation pattern of Russian military pistol was produced only in 1735, ten years after Peter's death.

Officers provided their own pistols, and Russian museums contain numerous examples of finely crafted and decorated weapons of foreign manufacture designed for military use. Many feature the baroque style decoration popular elsewhere in Europe. Unlike the majority of the troopers' pistols, these weapons had brass rather than iron fittings.

The Tsar's desire to gain an edge in firepower over the Swedes resulted in the use of a number of experimental firearms. A handful of twin-barrelled and twin rotating-lock pistols were employed on active service, the products of Dutch gunsmiths. These proved too fragile for military use, despite their increased rate of fire, and they were never supplied to the army in any numbers.

The large variety of firearm calibres found among both infantry and dragoons created a supply problem of epic proportions, a problem which bedevilled the Russian commissariat throughout the 18th century. As late as the Napoleonic wars, the Russian army was reported to possess 28 different calibres of small arms. References by a foreign ambassador to 'indifferently equipped dragoons' in 1705 might reflect both the slow progress made in the changeover to flintlock weapons and the multiplicity of calibres.

Swords

Although Petrine cavalry doctrine placed great emphasis on firepower, Russian dragoons were also trained to use *l'arme blanche*. Pre-Petrine cavalry for the most part carried sabres, either of Turkish or Polish-Hungarian forms; both types were fashionable in Russia, and were copied by Russian swordsmiths. Caucasian and Turkish influence produced Russian 'oriental' sabres of the '*gaddareh*' type, with comparatively short blades of flowing damascene steel with a wide back edge, a secret of production unknown to other European armourers.

Tsar Peter's dragoons of 1699–1700 were equipped with straight-bladed sidearms, both smallswords and broadswords. These were similar to swords found in Western armies, with a large number of blades imported from Germany (mostly from

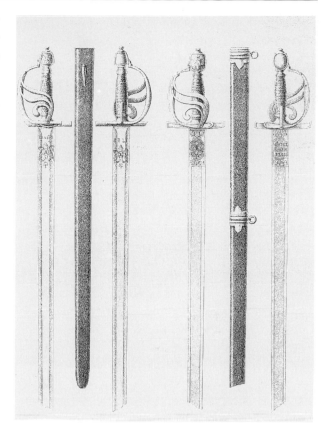

▼ *Dragoon swords (palashii) of 1700–32. The weapon on the left represents the type carried by officers and has a brass hilt with a steel-wire bound grip. The two views of a broadsword with shellguard show the weapon produced in the Olonetz factory in 1710. (Viskovatov)*

▶ *Dragoon swords of 1700–25. The two broadswords depicted are of the bar-guard form with a single fuller, and represent copies of contemporary Western European patterns. Both weapons were produced in Olonetz between 1718 and 1721. (Viskovatov)*

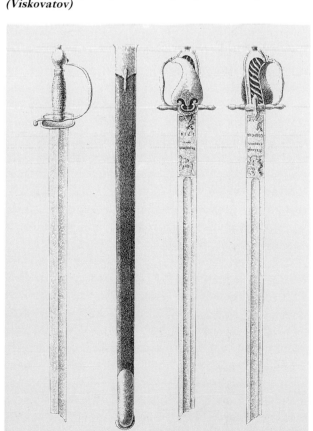

Solingen, the largest European production centre). Although dragoon officers carried larger versions of the smallswords carried by infantry officers, dragoon troopers were issued with broadswords having a wider two-edged or single-edged blade, used for both cutting and thrusting.

A large proportion of Russian-made swords were used, the principal production centre being Olonetz. No set pattern was adopted, some weapons having shell-guards and others bar-guards. Hilts were usually of gilded copper, and the handles wound with steel wire. Scabbards were of black leather with steel fittings.

Other equipment

Dragoon troopers were initially issued with a leather cartridge box (*patronnaya sumka*), suspended from a buff leather bandolier slung over the right shoulder. This was later replaced by a smaller box (*lyadunka*), modelled on that issued to Grenadiers. In some cases the bandolier was dispensed with and the *lyadunka* slung directly from the trooper's waistbelt (*portupeya*). A buff leather carbine sling was worn over the

Russian Dragoons at Poltava, with Tsar Peter at their head. Note the non-regulation officers' coats, and the kettle-drummer and trumpeter just visible on the left. Detail from an engraving by Larmessain after the painting by Martin the Younger, early 18th century. (State Historic Museum, Moscow)

left shoulder, with its sprung carbine hook (for attachment to a rail on the side of the carbine) hanging off the trooper's right hip. The sling was fastened at the rear by a brass buckle.

The leather saddle was placed over a shabraque (*cheprak*) in a colour of the regimental colonel's choosing, red predominating. Both saddle and *cheprak* were secured by a wide leather belly-strap. Large conical leather pistol holsters (*pistoletniye chushki*) were secured to the saddle by crossed leather straps. Two further sets of straps were suspended from the saddle; the stirrup leathers supporting an iron stirrup (*stremya*), and a carbine holster or shoe (*bushmat*), controlling the carbine suspended from the trooper's right side.

Garrison Dragoons

The formation of Garrison regiments to guard the frontier, occupy fortifications, assist in the administration of Russian provinces and to maintain law and order has been described in the companion volume, MAA 260. The Garrison corps was set up by an *ukas* of February 1712, and consisted of 39 infantry regiments and two Garrison Dragoon regiments (those of Voronezh and Kazan). In addition the Roslavl Dragoon Squadron was raised as a super-numerary police formation.

In 1716 two further Garrison Dragoon regiments were created (the Azov and Astrakhan regiments). Each formation served in the province which shared its regimental name, with the exception of the Roslavl Squadron, which was used for policing duties in and around Moscow, and the Voronezh Regiment, which was stationed in the Urals, attached to the Siberian provincial administration.

Each Garrison Dragoon regiment was organised into ten companies, each of approximately 100 men, with a total regimental strength of 1,077 officers and men, and 1,020 horses. The Roslavl Squadron consisted of five companies, with a total of 544 men and officers including squadron staff, and 526 horses.

These regiments were issued with dark green coats (*kaftans*) of an identical cut to those of Line dragoons, with red facings and red breeches. A collarless working coat of a rough grey cloth was worn beneath the *kaftan*. Boots, neckcloth and stockings were all identical to those supplied to Line Dragoon regiments. The 1720 dress regulations were introduced slowly, the majority of the Garrison regiments retaining their older pattern of uniform until after Tsar Peter's death.

CAVALRY STANDARDS

The defeat of the Russian army at Narva (1700) resulted in the loss of the majority of the army's standards, which were taken to Stockholm as trophies. These trophies form the main body of information on these early Petrine standards. Petrelli and Legrelius (1907) catalogued the surviving standards, and identified a number of them.

The Russian cavalry at Narva consisted of two Dragoon regiments, Goltz's and Schnewentz's, in addition to approximately 10,000 men of the old provincial cavalry regiments from Novgorod, Smolensk and Moscow. With the exception of the colonel's standards of the Dragoon regiments, all the captured cavalry standards were approximately 120 cm by 90 cm, a size more typical of Western infantry regiments. The size and design of Petrine Dragoon standards was to change several times.

The first basic design resembled that of Plate H1, the company standard of Schnewentz's Regiment having a gold cross on an ash-grey damask field with green palm leaves and bearing on a white scroll the Cyrillic inscription 'By this colour I shall triumph over my enemies'. Both colonel's standards had a double-headed crowned eagle, brown on a white field surrounded by green palm leaves for Goltz's Regiment. Both colonel's standards were surrounded by a fringe, of gold and red silk respectively.

The older provincial cavalry formations lost at least 125 standards at Narva, these falling into three main groups. The first group (21 standards) consisted of a yellow cross with gold rays surrounded by blue palm fronds on a light grey field. The inscription on a gold field was identical to that used by Goltz's

Regiment. A second group (54 standards) are described as being of various coloured damask, with long tails, and various highly decorative figures painted in gold and silver. The last group (46 standards) were white taffeta flags decorated with painted and dyed double-headed eagles, suns, moons and stars. All cavalry standards were mounted on brown staffs with silver or brass finials.

Following the post-Narva reforms, Dragoon regiments were each issued ten standards: one for the colonel's company and nine for the other companies (correspondingly more for the 12-company strong regiments created after 1704). These resembled the flags used by infantry regiments both in size and design—an unusual feature of the Petrine army, since most other European armies were by this time issuing their dragoon regiments with small, swallow-tailed standards (in effect, guidons). The sole feature distinguishing Russian infantry colours and dragoon standards was that the latter were edged with a 2 cm-wide gold fringe. The field of each company standard was coloured in the same manner as an infantry company flag, with each regiment using the same field colour as the infantry regiment sharing the same provincial title. These field colours are listed in the companion title, *Peter the Great's Army: 1*, p.40.

The colonel's standard of each Dragoon regiment had a white field (as in the infantry). The colonel's standards of all Dragoon regiments were, therefore, identical, though a number of surviving Petrine Dragoon company standards had the central gold chain device replaced with a cross, similar to the device on the captured Narva standards.

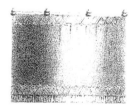

Russian kettledrum, c.1700–25; these were used by all Dragoon regiments. The copper drum was usually covered by a red fabric, edged in gold as shown in the upper illustration. (Viskovatov)

Table C: Dragoon standards, 1712 pattern

Regiment	Field colour	Regiment	Field colour
Moskovski	Red	Nizhegorodski	Green
Kievski	Red	Yaroslavski	Red, yellow band
Vladimirski	Black, blue triangle, green/red cross	Tverskoy	Red
		Permski	Red
Pskovski	Blue	Ingermanlandski	Black and yellow diagonals
Kazanski	Red	Nevski	Green
Novgorodski	Red	Ustiuzhski	Blue
Troitski	Red	Ryazanski	Yellow
Astrakhanski	Red, yellow band	Belozerski	Green and black cantons, green/blue cross
Sibirienski	Yellow		
Smolenski	Red	Arkhangelski	Blue
St. Petersburgski	Red	Luzhski	Yellow, red cross
Tschernigovski	Black	Vologodski	Red, black triangle, green/blue cross
Viatski	Black		

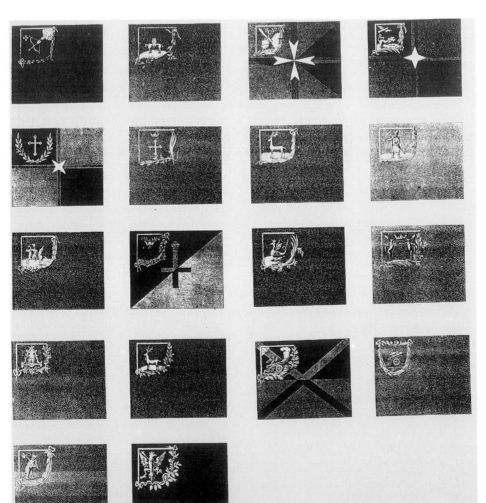

1712 pattern infantry flags. These were identical to the standards issued to the corresponding Dragoon regiments where these existed, except that Dragoon standards were surrounded by a narrow fringe. Top row (left to right): *Viatski, Permski, Vologodski, Belgorodski.* Second row: *Novotroitski, Troitski, Nizhegorodski, Ryazanski.* Third row: *Arkhangelski, Ingermanlandski, Kazanski, Sibirienski.* Fourth row: *Tverskoy, Rostovski, Voronezhski, Smolenski.* Fifth row: *Yaroslavski, Tschernigovski.* (Viskovatov)

Regiment	Field colour	Regiment	Field colour
Narvski	Black and red diagonal cantons, blue band	Kargopolski	Red
		Tobolski	Red, blue triangle, green and silver crosses
Rostovski	Blue		
Azovski	Yellow and red bands	Novotroitski	Black and red squares, green cross, gold star
Life Regt.	Red		
Olonetzski	Red, yellow cross		

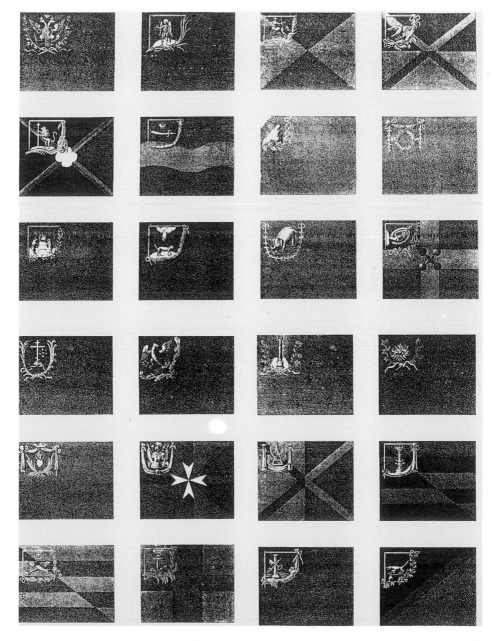

1712 pattern infantry flags continued. Top row (left to right): *Moskovski, Kievski, Boutyrski, Yamburgski.* Second row: *Vladimirski, Astrakhanski, Koporieschski, Life Rgt.* Third row: *Novgorodski, Pskovski, Vyborgski, Olonetzski.* Fourth row: *Lefort, Rentzel, Simbirski, Kargopolski.* Fifth row: *St. Petersburgski, Galitschski, Tobolski, Schlusselburgski.* Sixth row: *Azovski, Luzhski, Nevski, Narvski.* (Viskovatov)

A number of pre-Petrine cavalry regiments were retained for internal duties or used to form the cadres of new Dragoon regiments, so a number of earlier standards would have been retained until as late as 1712.

New pattern standards

The dragoon and infantry standards of the regular army were superseded by a new pattern, following an *ukas* of 25 October 1711; these were introduced in 1712. Henceforth each Dragoon regiment received a white colonel's colour displaying the monogram of Tsar Peter I in gold, surmounted by a gold crown. The monogram was surrounded by gold palm leaves intertwined with silver flowers. As before, the only difference between dragoon standards and infantry flags was the golden silk fringe edging the former. Each regiment received company standards in a distinctive regimental style with the motif of the province or town after which they were named; this was displayed in the top hoist canton, painted in 'natural' colours. The staff of the 1712 pattern dragoon standard was painted black, topped with a gold finial, and decorated with silver tassels. The standard itself measured 180 cm by 160 cm, excluding the gold silk fringe. The field colour for each regiment is shown in Table C.

GUARD CAVALRY

For the bulk of the Great Northern War, Tsar Peter rejected the extravagance of having an élite Guard cavalry formation, concentrating instead on the more practical Line Dragoon regiments. Despite this, both leading field commanders had squadron-sized escorts: the Life Squadron of Prince Menshikov and the General's Dragoon Company of Count Sheremetiev, both formed in 1704. These were trained as conventional cavalrymen rather than as dragoons. Composed largely of young officers, they were modelled on the Swedish Drabant Guard, although lacking the skill and *élan* of the Swedes.

The uniforms of both units were reportedly similar to those of the Line Dragoons, with Sheremetiev's company sporting red coats, and Menshikov's squadron having the same uniform colours as the Preobrazhenski Guard, to which they were affiliated for administrative purposes. Both units fought at Poltava, where they made up the only non-dragoon regular cavalry in Peter's army, with a combined strength of 220 troopers.

In 1719 the Tsar ordered that the two squadron-sized units be amalgamated with the dragoon company of the Governor of St. Petersburg, which had been formed in 1706 as a police unit for the capital. The resulting unit became the Life Regiment (of Life Guard Cavalry). Because of the hostile English fleet threatening the eastern Baltic, the amalgamation took place officially in March 1721, although the various squadrons had been brigaded together in St. Petersburg since the previous year. The regiment was at first referred to as the Kronslot Dragoon Regiment, becoming the Life Regiment on 27 April 1722. To prevent confusion a dragoon unit raised in 1707 and known as the Life Regiment, was renamed the St. Petersburgski Dragoon Regiment, the original St. Petersburgski Regiment having been disbanded in 1712 (see Table A, units 11 and 30).

A senior Russian officer pistolling a Swedish dragoon during the battle of Poltava (28 June 1709); the figure probably represents Count Sheremetiev. Both he and the troopers of his personal 'General's Dragoon Company' are depicted wearing red uniforms. Detail from Lomonsov's Poltava mosaic, mid-18th century. (The Hermitage Museum, St. Petersburg)

By this time the need for the regiment as an operational military formation had been replaced by the need for a training formation for young officers. The ranks of the regiment were already filled with young officers, and were expanded further by drafts of ambitious young noblemen. As the Life Regiment never left St. Petersburg, service within its ranks was regarded as a coveted military appointment. Troopers went on to become serving officers in Line Dragoon regiments.

Apart from training, the principal role of the Life Regiment was to perform ceremonial duties within the capital and its environs, and the regiment was used extensively on state occasions. Imperial escort duties to Peter the Great remained the prerogative of the infantry of the Preobrazhenski Guard Regiment.

The Life Regiment was later supplemented by the Company of Drabants (also referred to as the Chevalier Guard): this new mounted squadron was created on 31 March 1724, apparently at the request of the Empress Catherine for the occasion of her coronation. The all-officer squadron mustered 145 men, with the Emperor as their captain, and were used exclusively for state occasions. As such they were not administered by the College of War like the rest of the army. This unit was disbanded within a year, after Peter's death in January 1725.

LIGHT CAVALRY

When the regular cavalry arm was created, Tsar Peter opted to concentrate exclusively on raising dragoons. He considered that any duties undertaken by light cavalry in other European armies could be delegated in the Russian army either to Dragoons or to Cossacks. Although not unknown in Western armies, regular light cavalrymen were uncommon, and a relatively new military phenomenon. The success of Hungarian hussars serving with the Austrian army during the War of the Spanish Succession prompted other states to look into the formation of similar units.

When a series of rebellions against the Tsar's authority broke out amongst the Cossack hosts in 1707, Peter decided, as an experiment, to raise a regular light cavalry unit along Austrian lines. If successful, the unit was to be expanded, so overcoming the need for the often unreliable Cossacks.

Gentleman of the Life Regiment of Cavalry, part of the Russian Imperial Guard, c.1724. The uniform is similar to that worn by Line Dragoon officers, with the addition of a decorated surcoat. (Viskovatov)

Apostol Kigetsch, a Wallachian nobleman with active hussar experience, was appointed to raise the first *khorugv'* ('banner' or squadron) of 300 men, which was to be recruited mainly from the Christian communities in Hungary, Serbia, Moldavia and Wallachia. Once raised, the unit served along the edge of Cossack territory, on the Russian border with Turkish Wallachia, and acted as a border garrison force.

In time of war it was planned to use hussars to help offset the Ottoman superiority in irregular horsemen. Immediately before the Pruth campaign of 1711, the regular light cavalry were increased to six full regiments (each of four *khorugvi*, totalling 800 men); the majority of these new hussars were recruited from Wallachia. In addition two further *khorugvi*, one Polish and one Serbian, were raised from Christian volunteers especially for the impending war against the Turks.

These troops were employed in what would now

be classified as guerrilla warfare, their duties including reconnaissance, ambushes, surprise attacks and the harassment of supply lines. Specific instructions from the Tsar forbade any action against the local Wallachian population, as their liberation from the Turks was Peter's *raison de guerre*. However, these light troops proved to be of little value during the campaign, and most were disbanded soon afterwards, their high cost and poor discipline being cited as the reasons. Two units were retained—a Hungarian and a Wallachian hussar regiment—but these too were disbanded in 1721.

A second attempt was made to raise regular light cavalry in 1723, when Tsar Peter commissioned Major Albanes (a Serb already in Russian service) to form a hussar regiment. These hussars were recruited exclusively from Serbian light cavalry serving in the Austrian army. They were assigned permanent billets on the Ukrainian-Moldavian border, and were paid the same wages as they had received when in Austrian service. Only 340 men were raised for the regiment, and by 1725 the majority had returned either to Serbia or to Austrian service, only 94 still remaining in Russia.

As a troop type, regular light cavalry never proved their worth to the Tsar; and as administrative control over the Cossack hosts tightened the requirement for other light cavalry diminished. No details have been uncovered of the uniforms of the short-lived Russian hussar formations, though these were probably similar to dress worn in Austrian service: a fur pelisse, a braided tunic, high boots and a fur cap.

COSSACKS

When Tsar Alexis Mikhailovich, Peter's father, took Kiev and the fertile region along both banks of the Dniepr from the Poles, he established Muscovite Russia as the nominal protector of the Ukrainian Cossacks. The origin of the term 'cossack' (*kazak*) is obscure; but what began as the movement of oppressed serfs and outlaws into unclaimed territory had, by the late 17th century, become a collection of self-administering communities located on the southern boundaries of Muscovite Russia. As such they formed a buffer between Russia and the Tatars, and proved a valuable ally when Russia engaged in campaigns against the Poles and Turks.

A quasi-military caste, these Cossack communities (or 'hosts') comprised a mixture of ethnic groups (though not a mixture of religious beliefs). By the reign of Tsar Peter they were in the midst of a process of amalgamation into the Russian state, while still maintaining a substantial degree of autonomy; though their traditionally independent nature was becoming increasingly difficult to reconcile with the growing centralisation of power.

Although all the Cossack hosts had similar

Fuzeler *(trooper) of a Line Dragoon regiment, c.1720–25. He wears the post-1720 pattern uniform, and his carbine sling is* worn correctly over the sling of the cartridge box. St. Petersburg is depicted in the background. (Viskovatov)

Narva, 1700:
Noble cavalry
1: Boyar commander
2: Muscovite metropolitan cavalryman
3, 4: Smolensk provincial cavalrymen

A

Lesnaya, 1708:
1, 2: Troopers, Vladimirski Dragoon Regt.
3: Captain, Moskovski Dragoon Regt.
4, 5: Troopers, Moskovski Dragoon Regt.

B

Poltava, 1709:
1: Trooper, Ingermanlandski Dragoon Regt.
2: Trooper, Kropotov's Horse Grenadier Regt.
3: Drummer, Ingermanlandski Dragoon Regt.
4: Ensign, Ingermanlandski Dragoon Regt.

1

2

Lithuania, 1721:
1, 2: Troopers, Line Dragoon Regt.
3: Trooper, Dragoon Garrison Regt.
4: Ensign, Line Dragoon Regt.

D

3

4

Vyborg, 1710:
Artillery Regiment
1: Bombardier
2, 3: Cannoniers
4: Junior Officer

1   2   3   4   E

St. Petersburg, 1724:
Life Guard Cavalry
1: Trooper, Life Regt.
2: Major, Life Regt.
3: Prince Menshikov

F

3

2

1

Stockholm, 1719:
1: Don Cossack
2: Don Cossack commander
3: Kalmuk horseman

G

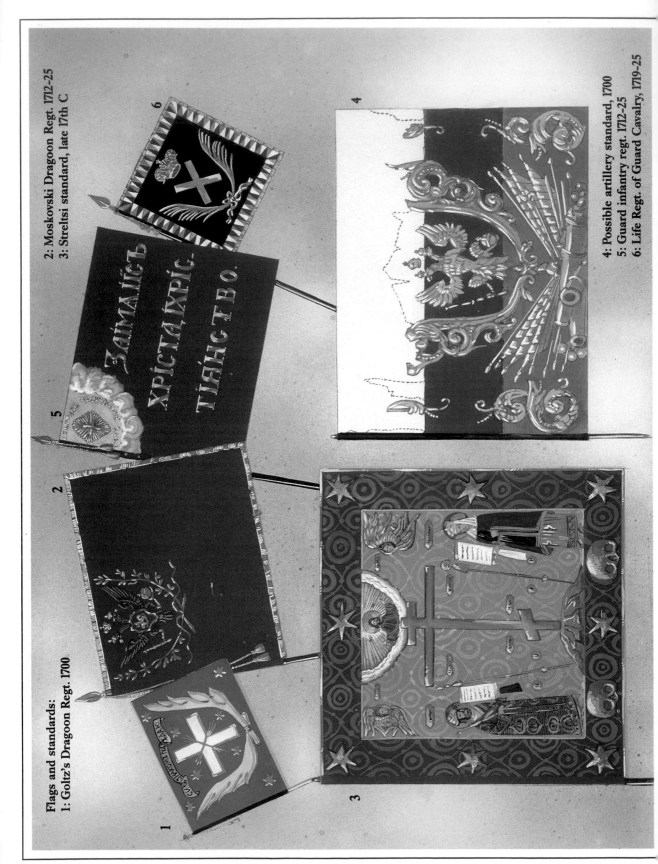

Flags and standards:
1: Goltz's Dragoon Regt. 1700

2: Moskovski Dragoon Regt. 1712-25
3: Streltsi standard, late 17th C

4: Possible artillery standard, 1700
5: Guard infantry regt. 1712-25
6: Life Regt. of Guard Cavalry, 1719-25

H

origins and were subjected to broadly similar external pressures, each host retained its own geographical and political characteristics:

The *Ukrainian Cossacks* were located on the upper Dniepr River, and formed the largest of the Cossack communities. These 'Little Russians' replaced the overlordship of the Polish Crown with that of the Tsar, and by the reign of Tsar Peter were becoming increasingly dominated by Russia. Their *hetman* or *ataman* ('leader'), Mazeppa was torn between loyalty to the Tsar, dreams of independence in the wake of a Swedish victory, and the desire of his people to live in peace. They could field a host of about 20,000 riders.

The *Zaporozhian Cossacks* were based on islands amidst the rapids of the lower Dniepr River (*za parohy* means 'beyond the cataracts'). Less Russian-influenced than the Ukrainian Cossacks, they remained the most loyal of all the hosts to the independent Cossack spirit. Their defended settlement (*sech*) formed the hub of their social and military community. Their host was estimated at around 15,000 men.

The *Don Cossacks* inhabited the lower Don River basin, from Voronezh to Azov. Their proximity to Crimean Tatar territory fostered close links with Moscow, and throughout the 17th century they co-operated in Russian campaigns against the Turks. Despite frequently heavy-handed treatment by Russia they contributed the most consistently reliable Cossack element to Tsar Peter's army. It was Don Cossack *sotnias* that were most often used during campaigns in Livonia, Poland, Germany and Sweden. Their total military strength has been put at 15,000 men.

The *Terek Cossacks* (or Black Sea Cossacks) occupied the Kuban, isolated from direct Russian influence by intervening Tatar territory. They participated in Tsar Peter's campaigns in the Caucasus, at which time Russian control over them was established.

The *Yaik Cossacks* (or Ural Cossacks) were the remnant of earlier Cossack groups who formerly attempted to found settlements in Siberia. Despite the establishment of an increasing number of Russian industrial settlements in the Urals, these maintained their independence throughout Tsar Peter's reign.

The Cossack Rebellions

The Don Revolt

In 1700 Tsar Peter ordered the Don Cossacks to return runaway serfs escaping military conscription. When the Don *ataman* refused, Russian troops occupied the upper Don basin, establishing a cordon between Cossacks and serfs. In 1706, Prince Dolgo-ruki led a punitive expedition into the Cossack lands using former *streltsi* and noble cavalry regiments. His force was ambushed by rebel Don Cossacks led by Kondrati Bulavin, the Russian troops were massac-

This stylised representation of a Don Cossack shows the essentials of early 18th century Cossack attire: kaftan, baggy trousers and boots. Although his sabre is of Western origin, the firearm is a Caucasian 'snaphaunce' musket. (Viskovatov)

red and Dolgoruki killed. Bulavin then fled to the Zaporozhians, who rose in support. Returning to the Don, he defeated loyal Cossacks and proclaimed himself *ataman*. Tsar Peter sent a second expedition to crush the revolt, which forced the rebels to disperse. Many rebels fled to the Kuban to join the Terek Cossacks, and Bulavin committed suicide. The Don Cossacks remained under firm Russian control for the remainder of Peter's reign.

The Ukrainian Revolt

When Hetman Mazeppa negotiated an alliance with Charles XII, many of his Cossacks retained their allegiance to the Tsar. Prince Menshikov led a *korvolan* to the Ukrainian Cossack capital of Baturin ahead of the Swedes, crushing the rebellion and forcing Mazeppa to flee with a few hundred suppor-

ters. The Ukrainian Cossacks deposed him and appointed Ivan Skoropadsky as the new *hetman*.

Although Skoropadsky did as the Tsar requested, Peter was distrustful of the loyalty of both *hetman* and his host. At one point he is reputed to have said 'from Khmelnitsky to Skoropadsky, all Ukrainian *hetmen* have been traitors'. On Skoropadsky's death new *hetmen* were appointed directly by the Tsar; and from 1722 all Ukrainian affairs fell under the jurisdiction of the College of War.

The rebel Mazeppa found supporters among the Zaporozhians, but following Poltava he joined Charles XII in exile in Turkey, where he died. Those of his supporters captured after Poltava were killed 'in such ways as rebels are executed'.

The Zaporozhian Revolt

The Tsar saw the Zaporozhian Cossacks as the greatest threat to his new suzerainty over the Cossack hosts. While Charles XII was gathering his forces for the siege of Poltava, a Russian expedition was sent against the Zaporozhians in the lower Dniepr, and in May 1709 the *sech* was besieged and razed. Although the Zaporozhian community was never completely tamed during Peter's reign, any major Zaporozhian threat to Russia's stability was eradicated.

Cossack organisation

The Cossacks saw themselves as a military people, and the entire political structure of each host was organised as an army (*voisko*). Each host was sub-divided into 'regiments' which were administrative areas, each responsible for the raising of a regiment-sized military force. For example the Ukrainian host consisted of the Akhtirski, Chernigovski, Izyumski, Kharkovski, Kievski, Severski and Sumski regiments, which were both territorial centres and military units. Each regiment was in turn organised into *sotnias* ('hundreds', the equivalent of squadrons or companies), each theoretically consisting of 100 Cossacks, but often numbering over 200. These were further sub-divided into *kurens* (troops) of 25–40 men.

Commander of a Cossack sotnia, *from the time of Peter the Great. His stylised attire resembles that of the previous figure, but with a longer blue* kaftan *and decorated waistbelt. Both Cossacks wear blue cloth caps trimmed with fur. (Viskovatov)*

Each *voisko* was administered by an assembly which in theory appointed the *ataman* or *hetman*. As all Cossacks were nominally in Russian service from the late 17th century, and were paid 5 roubles per annum, the Tsar was entitled to approve the choice of an *ataman*. From the 1720s he appointed them himself, through the College of War set up partly to administer Cossack affairs. By the end of Peter's reign regular Russian officers were appointed to Cossack regiments on active service.

The Cossack character

Much has been made of the Cossack cavalry, immortalised in the works of Gogol, Pushkin and Sholokov (incidentally, the three authors also reflect the increasing influence of Russian authority). While maintaining a degree of independence of action, their loyalty first to their community and *ataman* and then to the Tsar placed some degree of constraint upon their activities.

A later British observer saw them as 'a cruel horde of plunderers, preying alike on friends and foes … never restrained in their actions by an inconvenient sense of moral obligations' (Austin, quoted in Brett-Jones (Ed.), 1964). More generous reports describe them as 'a very strong and indefatigable people' (Rondeau, 1736). This freebooting tendency could be harnessed by the Russian military to serve a useful purpose. During Sheremetiev's Livonian campaign of 1701–2 Cossacks were used to ravage the countryside, an employment repeated during Apraxin's raids on the Swedish mainland in 1719 and 1720.

Cossacks rode small, tough horses of up to $14\frac{1}{2}$ hands (58 inches), descended from those found on the Asiatic steppes; what they lacked in strength they made up for in stamina, being capable of travelling long distances on poor rations. Each Cossack normally had a second horse or pony used to carry provisions or plunder. On extended service, supply waggons would accompany Cossack regiments.

As a greater degree of military control came to be exercised over the hosts the required weaponry of a Cossack on state service was laid down as: a sabre, at least one pistol, and a musket (often long-ranged rifled pieces of Caucasian design, known colloquially as '*Turki*'). If possible a lightweight lance would be carried, of 2 *sazhen* (4.5 metres) in length. The Cossacks' loose riding styles, their high saddles, and their frequent absence of spurs, contrasted them with the regular dragoons of the Russian army.

Regulated uniforms do not appear to have been issued, though characteristic clothing gave the Cossacks their distinctive appearance. Kaftans and baggy trousers tucked into boots or Turkish shoes appear to have been commonly worn. Ukrainian and Zaporozhian Cossacks favoured a modified short *kaftan* (*chekmen*), while Yaik Cossacks wore a heavier coat and are depicted in later illustrations with fur headgear. Viskovatov's stylised illustrations depict other Cossack groups wearing round red or white caps trimmed with fur.

Further depiction of a Dragoon wearing the 1720 pattern uniform; the sheathed smallsword is incorrect. (Viskovatov)

The established military role for Cossacks in Tsar Peter's army was as scouts, ambushers, harriers and pursuers. An English officer attached to Charles XII's army records the effect of this constant harassment: 'I cannot describe to Y:r Hon:r the great vigilance of owr ennemys, who use all the methods of the most experienc'd soldiers to allarm us, and keep us for the most part both day and night, with one foot in the stirrup, these continuall fatigues and the want of provision which begins more and more to press us has allready occasion'd murmerings in the army, and will be of worse consequence if shortly there be not some alteration for the better' (Hatton, 1954).

In combat Cossacks rode towards the enemy in an extended line, attempting to envelop the enemy force. Bellicose posturing and shouting (traditionally, '*urrah!*') were used to intimidate, playing on the Cossacks' reputation for ferocity. In the face of any organised opposition the Cossack force retired, ready to repeat the attack when the opportunity offered. Englund (1992) describes one such attack, launched during a Swedish regimental sermon on the eve of the battle of Poltava: 'Westerman [the chaplain] was not allowed to conduct his service in peace this morning. A band of Russian Cossacks appeared in the middle of the sermon. They rode in, shouting and shooting,

and finally arrived a few hundred paces from the Swedish bivouacs. Some of the Zaporozhnians allied to the Swedes rode into the attack on the intruders, who allowed themselves to be driven off without great difficulty.'

Asiatic irregular cavalry

On occasion the Russian army hired non-Cossack irregular horsemen from the outer fringes of Russia: Kalmuks from the area around Astrakhan, and Bashkirs from the Urals. Both Sheremetiev and Apraxin used them during their raids on Swedish territory, where it was hoped that their Asiatic appearance would have an effect on the morale of the local population. These nomadic horsemen still used composite bows as late as the 19th century. Peter Henry Bruce, who visited Russia in the 18th century, wrote of their appearance: 'They are of low stature, and are generally bow-legged, occasioned by their being so continually on horseback, or sitting with their legs below them. Their faces are broad and flat, with a flat nose and little black eyes, distant from each other like the Chinese. They are of an olive colour, and their faces full of wrinkles, with very little or no beard. They shave their heads, leaving only a tuft of hair on the crown.'

A Kalmuk depicted mounted on a cow, with small Asiatic agrarian settlement in the background. His armament of a composite bow and oriental quiver corresponds with Bruce's account of these Asiatic horsemen. (Author's collection)

ARTILLERY

Artillery had long played an important role in the armies of Muscovite Russia. Despite the transport problems inherent in a vast country covered with forests and endless grasslands, the Muscovites concentrated on the production of large guns, the main value of artillery being seen as in siege warfare. A sizeable siege train was built up during the intermittent wars with Poland. Examples of these pieces are now displayed at the Moscow Kremlin.

During the late 17th century the state foundry in the Moscow Kremlin was overseen by the master founder Martin Osumov. The bronze guns cast by him formed the bulk of the artillery train inherited by Tsar Peter, and were employed at the sieges of Azov (1696) and Narva (1700). Contemporary illustrations of artillery used by Peter's *poteshnye* ('play') regiments give an indication of the types of carriages on which these pieces were mounted, the carriages being painted brick red or ochre. Although no identifiable early Petrine gun carriages remain, a near-contemporary artillery model in the State Artillery Museum, St. Petersburg, shows a bronze decorated barrel cast by Osumov mounted on a carriage resembling those illustrated in late-17th century artillery treatises. The foreign advisers hired by Tsar Alexis included artillery specialists, so similarities to Western examples are not surprising.

A further centre of artillery production in Russia was outside direct state control: the Ukrainian Cossacks produced their own guns at their foundry in Kiev. Their bronze barrels bear the mark of their *hetman*, Mazeppa. Almost all surviving Ukrainian pieces have an animal cast in relief on the right side of the barrel.

At the battle of Narva (1700) the Russian artillery train consisted of four 30- and 48-pdr guns; 26 × 18- and 24-pdrs; 33 × 6-, 10- and 12-pdrs; and 50 × 3-pdrs. There were also 25 × 80- and 120-pdr mortars, and one 40-pdr howitzer. The performance of these guns in the battle was poor: they were badly sited, the crews were raw, carriages broke when guns were fired, and many of the mortars lacked bombs of a suitable size. Not surprisingly the entire train was captured. The train's commander was General Field-Quartermaster Prince Alexander Artschilovitsch of

Artillery and mortars participating in the exercises of Peter's 'poteshnye' (play) regiments outside Preobrazhenskoe. All carriages are shown painted in an orange-red colour. Watercolour from Krekshnin's History of Tsar Peter I. (The Lenin Library, Moscow)

Imertia, who had studied gunnery at the Hague in 1698–9; he was replaced after the battle.

Artillery reorganisation

Following Narva, organisational reform of the artillery train, which had begun on a small scale in 1699, was put into effect in earnest. Artillery were grouped into *ad hoc* batteries for field, fortress and siege use. These units were consolidated by the regulation of

1701 into a regiment of artillery, the ranks of which included gunners, bombardiers, miners, engineers, pontoniers and pioneers.

Since 1697, the Preobrazhenski Guard Regiment had contained a 'bombardier' detachment armed with six 6-pdr Coehorn mortars and four 3-pdr regimental guns; similarly, the Semenovski Guard Regiment's cannonier command comprised six 3-pdrs. As at Narva, all other infantry regiments were issued with two 3-pdr guns. The use of regimental artillery continued throughout the Great Northern War.

The Artillery Regiment audit of 8 February 1712 produces a complete organisational record: 1 bombardier coy. (113 men); 6 cannonier coys. (152 men each); 1 miner coy. (75 men); plus 25 engineers, 36 pioneers (pontooniers), 6 petardiers and 19 staff. These companies were purely administrative in nature. Bombardiers served the howitzers and mortars, the cannoniers served the ordinary artillery pieces. Both carried firearms: the cannoniers had muskets, and the bombardiers hand mortars which could fire grenades weighing just under one Russian pound, and rested on artillery halberds when firing (see Plate E1).

At Poltava (1709), the train consisted of: 68×3-pdrs (regimental guns); 13×2-pdrs (horse artillery); 12×8-pdrs; 2×12-pdrs; $2 \times$ howitzers (a 20-pdr and a 40-pdr); 1×20-pdr mortar; and 2×40-pdr mortars.

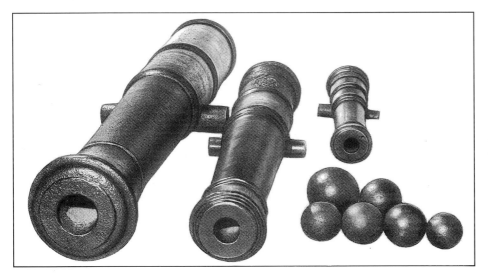

Artillery pieces from the reign of Tsar Peter. The 12-pdr on the left is a naval cast-iron piece, while the bronze 6-pdr and 3-pdr are designed for use by the artillery train. (State Artillery Museum, St. Petersburg)

A model of a pre-Petrine Russian bronze field piece. The mouldings and other features resemble existing barrels; it is mounted on a contemporary Russian carriage. The model has been dated to the late 17th century. (State Historic Museum, Moscow)

In 1723 the train of non-regimental guns ('the chief artillery') excluding siege guns was recorded as consisting of: 6 × 6-pdrs; 12 × 8-pdrs; 3 × 12-pdrs; and 4 × 20-pdr mortars. In addition there were 80 × 3-pdr regimental guns. The full siege train inventoried in 1723 contained: 30 × 18-pdrs; 30 × 24-pdrs; and 100 Coehorn mortars.

Peter also experimented with horse artillery. From 1706, each Dragoon regiment in theory had a detachment of two 2-pdr light howitzers, with crews mounted on riding horses. This project was only partially implemented by the battle of Poltava, and was abandoned soon after due to technical problems.

Bruce's reforms

Count James William Bruce, the grandson of a Scottish émigré who came to Russia in the mid-17th century, was, as the Field-Quartermaster General of Artillery (General of Ordnance), perhaps the most influential figure involved in the reorganisation of Peter's artillery. One of his first acts was to create the Artillery Regiment, and he went on to separate field and siege artillery. He standardised the artillery poundage system, so that one Russian pound (0.4 kg or 96 *zolotniks*) equated to a 5 cm iron ball.

He supervised the proofing of new barrels and worked closely with founders on improvements to barrel design and quality, assisted by his production of accurate barrel plans and dimensions. One of his major achievements was the reduction of barrel weight, so that a 12-pdr was reduced from 112 to 30 *pud* (1 *pud* = 40 Russian pounds). Carriages were also lightened, with the aim of improving both strength and mobility. All carriage components were to be built according to set specifications (measured in calibres), so creating a uniform range of carriages. Colours of carriages varied, but by 1720 a brick red had become the standard. Bruce's detailed specifications for both guns and carriages were to create one of the earliest successful 'artillery systems' in Europe.

Artillery production

The army's most pressing need in 1701 was to replace the artillery lost at Narva. Traditionally, such shortages had been remedied by collecting bronze church bells from all over Russia to be melted down and recast as artillery barrels. As a result of Peter's

James William Bruce (1670–1735), General of Ordnance in Peter's army. Many of his reforms of the Russian artillery arm were revolutionary in nature; he commanded the artillery with success at Poltava and at a number of sieges, including Vyborg. Engraving by anonymous German artist, c. 1710. (State Historic Museum, Moscow)

contacts with the West new technology was brought to Russia; this combined with an increasingly efficient exploitation of Russia's vast natural resources to give considerable improvements in artillery production. The existing works at Tula (set up in 1632 by Dutch experts) were enlarged, and new metal foundries were created in the Urals, where the latest mechanical devices were used to speed production. The abundance of ore and timber in the Urals allowed for a large production of iron-ore, used to cast naval guns. Completed barrels were shipped by river to Moscow and St. Petersburg.

Because of the difficulties of transport, further local foundries were established at St. Petersburg and Olonetz (bronze) and Petrozavodsk (iron). These regions produced a steady flow of artillery and shot for both the army and the fleet. Powder factories were set up at Ochta and Sestroryetsk. By the 1720s Russia was self-sufficient in all war materials, and was even producing a surplus for export.

Artillery uniforms

Artillerymen were dressed in a similar fashion to the infantry. Coats, vests and breeches were red, with cornflower blue cuff turnbacks and buttonhole-linings. Stockings were either blue or white with blue vertical stripes. Both the tricorne and the *kartuz* could be worn, the latter of red wool with a blue lining. A black neckcloth and a cornflower blue overcoat completed the uniform issue. Bombardiers wore a mitre cap similar to that of Guard Grenadiers, but without a plume.

From 1720 the uniform was changed to the 1720-pattern red coat with a red falling collar, with blue cuff turnbacks and buttonhole linings. The vest and trousers were red, with a white neckcloth, and stockings of white wool. A cornflower blue overcoat and black tricorne trimmed white were also issued.

Though the dress of officers was still not specified, regulations suggested that these resemble those of the men with the exception of the cuffs which were to be red, with gold trim. Sashes should be worn as by infantry officers. It is worth noting that artillery officers were held in high regard, and were rated and paid one rank higher than their actual rank.

MILITARY ADMINISTRATION

At the start of the Great Northern War Tsar Peter's military administration was minimal. He was accompanied by a small field chancellery (*blizhnyana pokhodnaya kantselyariya*) through which he administered both the army and the state. Aside from his military staff this body included commissars and quartermasters who channelled drafts of recruits received from Russia's local military governors.

This provincial administration was achieved in 1709 by dividing the country into eight military districts (*gubernii*), each ruled by a military governor invested with extensive military and civil powers. Each *gubernia* was responsible for the billeting and provisioning of regiments stationed within its boundaries. The declining threat from Sweden allowed a

more formal system to be instituted as the Tsar was able to devote more time to administrative matters.

In 1711 Tsar Peter set up the Senate, an executive body directed to control the war effort and the raising of taxes on the Tsar's behalf. In the same year the eight *gubernii* (Moscow, St. Petersburg, Kiev, Smolensk, Archangel, Kazan, Azov and Siberia) were remodelled on Swedish lines by subdividing the districts into provinces (*provintsii*), each ruled by a provincial administrator (*voevoda*), with military and fiscal duties including recruiting, taxation and the obtaining of army provisions.

Within a few years this system showed signs of collapse, as corruption and inefficiency hindered the flow of revenue, men and *matériel* to St. Petersburg. By 1719 this administration had largely fallen under military control, and the country was re-divided into regimental districts. In many cases the army not only assisted the *voevodas* but replaced them. By 1725 the army gathered provisions and taxes directly, raised recruits and maintained law and order. The articles of war applied to the entire population, so that by the time of Peter's death the country was effectively under military law.

Towards the end of the war the Tsar established a collegiate system of administration on the Swedish model. This replaced the informal councils of war (*prikazy*) in the upper levels of military administration. Thus from 1719 the War College (or ministry) oversaw the administration of the whole army. It consisted of a President (or Minister of War), several councillors and assessors, administrative officials and a treasurer. The whole system operated on lines laid down by the Tsar in his War Regulations, part of the Military Code of 1716. Opportunities for corruption were reduced by the use of committees and a body of independent assessors.

The result was an army administration which was regarded as one of the best in Europe. The involvement of the military in all levels of the fiscal and administrative process ensured that the state would safeguard the needs of the Russian army.

The Army Commissariat

Although Peter's first army was poorly catered for in administration, it boasted a small commissariat, led by a Commissar General, assisted by a Senior Commissar, Pay Commissar and an Auditor. The

Military Code of 1716 reorganised this under a General War Commissar who held the treasury for pay and provisioning, and who ran the army accounts. Under him were two Chief War Commissars, one each for the infantry and dragoons. Each major body of troops (of divisional size) had a Chief War Commissar attached.

The military code outlined the provisioning requirements of the army, supplied through the *provintsii* system. Each soldier received an annual provision of 3 *tschetverti* (or 50 bucketfuls) of flour, $1\frac{1}{2}$ *tschetverti* of oats, 24 pounds of salt and 75 kopeks worth of meat. A horse was rationed to 6 *tschetverti* of oats and 90 pounds of hay every six months. On active campaign beyond the *provintsii* boundaries, daily rations in theory consisted of 2 pounds of bread and one of meat, and 2 glasses of spirits; in addition there was a monthly allowance of salt. When stationed in *provintsii*, supplies were often financial rather than actual, officers receiving higher allocations according to rank. Pay was issued through the Commissariat, after deductions had been made for food and clothing (approximately half of the pay of privates and NCOs). The annual pay for all ranks in 1712 is shown in Table D.

The cost of feeding the average soldier was estimated at 5 roubles a year, which was deducted from pay. In addition, uniform costs were deducted at a set rate, with each item having an expected life. The figures illustrate the low cost of uniforms, which

▲ *General-Admiral Apraxin (1661–1728). 'Father of the Russian navy', he masterminded the defence of St. Petersburg and the capture of Finland, despite twice being dismissed for corruption. Anonymous artist, early 18th century. (State Historic Museum, Moscow)*

▶ *Plan of the siege of the Finnish fortress town of Vyborg (1710). Apraxin's siege lines and approach saps are seen in the upper left, and the location of Bruce's siege battery is to the right of the town. Orientation is with south to the top of the plan. Engraving by Zubov, The Book of Mars, 1713. (State Historic Museum, Moscow)*

were essentially a fairly smart but uncomfortable costume.

By 1720 the army was costing the state approximately 4,000,000 roubles a year, 1,243,000 roubles of this being spent on provisions and fodder. This was almost double the cost of the army in 1711, an increase explained partly by army expansion and the cost of improved uniforms and equipment. The costs of individual items of uniform are shown in Table E.

The clothing of Garrison troops was even cheaper: for each man in a Baltic province garrison the total cost was 2:11 roubles, and for other garrisons 1:83 roubles. The clothing of Garrison Dragoons cost 2:77 roubles per man. The cost of outfitting and equipping the Petrine army was substantially lower than that of other European states. This allowed Russia to replace manpower losses without incurring a crippling financial penalty.

However, supplies of clothing were erratic and the effects were sometimes less than ideal. The English Ambassador Whitworth reported, in 1705 that: 'The two regiments of Guards and that of Ingermanland are well armed and clothed, though most of the rest are but indifferently provided with habits and firearms'.

THE PLATES

A: Narva, 1700

King Charles XII of Sweden's victory over the raw Russian army gave the Swedes a contemptuous disregard for Peter's troops. Much of this was based on the poor performance of the noble cavalry, who fled as the Swedes approached, many being drowned in the River Narva.

A1: Boyar, noble cavalry commander

This figure wears a buffcoat, a Western garment that became popular in Eastern Europe in the 17th century. The original is in the Royal Armouries, Tower of London. His coat is derived from contemporary illustrations of Russian nobles. The horse furnishings are based upon an example in the Kremlin Armoury.

A2: Muscovite metropolitan noble cavalryman

These cavalrymen considered themselves the élite of the noble cavalry military corps. The uniform has been slightly 'Westernised' through the influence of the Tsar's reforms and the many Western military advisers in Russia. His armament consists of weapons now in the Kremlin armoury.

A3, 4: Smolensk provincial noble cavalrymen

The *kaftan* resembles those of the Streltsi regiments, and is of traditional Russian design. These figures are loosely based on Muscovite cavalrymen depicted in Swedish propaganda engravings of the battle, such as the illustration of Charles XII at Narva. The original weapons are in the Kremlin Armoury, and the Livrustkammaren, Stockholm.

Table D: Annual pay in roubles, 1712

Rank	Foreigner	Russian	Garrison soldier
Gen. Field-Marshal		7,000	
General	3,600	3,120	
Lt. General	2,160	1,800	
Major General	1,800	1,080	
Brigadier		840	
Colonel	600	300	150
Lt. Colonel	360	150	75
Major	300	140	70
Captain	216	100	50
Lieutenant	120	80	40
Ensign, Sergeant		14.39	7.7
Corporal		13.66	6.28
Private		12	4

Table E: Uniform costs (in roubles: kopeks)

Item	Infantry	Dragoons	Wear-out time (years)
Headgear	0:21	0:21	2
Coat	3:41	3:33	3
Vest	2:43	3:50	3
Overcoat	3:65	3:65	$3\frac{1}{2}$
Neckcloth	0:03	0:03	$1\frac{1}{2}$
Shoes/Boots	0:54	0:94	1
Stockings (2 pairs)	0:30	0:30	1
Shirts (2 pairs)	0:30	0:30	1
Overstockings	0:16	0:16	1

B: Lesnaya, 1708
This hard-won Russian victory, which has been described as 'the mother of Poltava', involved the ambush of a Swedish army by a *korvolan* (flying corps) of dragoons and infantry commanded by Tsar Peter.

B1, 2: Troopers, Vladimirski Dragoon Regiment
Each dragoon wears the 1700–20 pattern *kaftan* and a *kartuz* cap. The dragoon's smaller cartridge box was issued as supplies permitted, and often the infantry model was used instead. His heavy cavalry boots could be turned up for wear when mounted. When dismounted, Russian dragoons normally fought in close order, though they could adopt a skirmish role when terrain and circumstances demanded. The armament is based upon examples from the Kremlin Armoury.

B3: Captain, Moskovski Dragoon Regiment
Under-officers were not constrained to wear the same uniform as their troopers. The overcoat colours of the Moskovski Regiment are among the few recorded. This officer is depicted wearing such an overcoat over his white regimental *kaftan*, while his sash identifies his rank. On campaign officers armed themselves with firearms at their own expense, such as this Dutch cavalry pistol.

B4, 5: Troopers, Moskovski Dragoon Regiment
These troopers wear the *treugolka* (tricorne) favoured by the majority of Dragoon regiments. The 1700–20 pattern *kaftan* is of a colour chosen by the regimental commander. Both the shortened musket and sword are displayed in the State Historic Museum, Moscow.

C: Poltava, 1709
The decisive battle of the Great Northern war, Poltava began and ended with cavalry engagements. During the closing stages of the battle Russian dragoons supported their infantry by conducting repeated attacks on the isolated Swedish foot. Their

Russian artillery linstock, early 18th century. The jaws are formed to represent bear heads, while the central head is engraved with the monogram of Tsar Peter I. (State Artillery Museum, St. Petersburg)

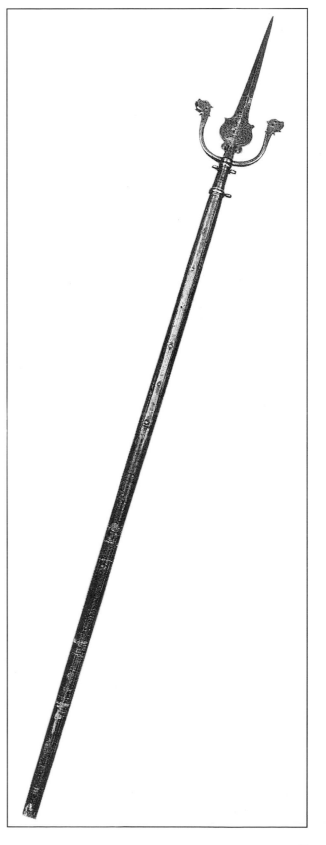

intervention prevented the majority of the Swedes from extricating themselves to fight another day.

C1: Trooper, Ingermanlandski Dragoon Regiment
The trooper carries a Russian-made carbine suspended from his carbine sling and is firing a Dutch flintlock pistol (originals in the State Historic Museum). He is equipped with a cartridge box of the infantry pattern, slung from his right shoulder.

C2: Trooper, Kropotov's Horse Grenadier Regiment
Horse Grenadiers wore an almost identical uniform to their infantry counterparts, the *kaftan* and mitre in the colour of the colonel's choosing; Von der Ropp's grenadiers wore red mitres and *kaftans*, and those of Roshnov's Regiment wore green. Grenade boxes were not officially issued to Horse Grenadier regiments, as the throwing of grenades from horseback was considered impractical.

C3: Drummer, Ingermanlandski Dragoon Regiment
Dragoon drummers differed from those of foot regiments only by their cavalry boots, although Dragoon regiments also included kettle drummers and trumpeters in their ranks. The drum was identical to the infantry version, and was designed for use when dismounted rather than when on horseback. The drum has been slung, and the drummer is wielding a dragoon broadsword.

C4: Ensign, Ingermanlandski Dragoon Regiment
The flag carried by this junior officer is of the large dragoon pattern used between 1700 and 1712. The white colour denotes the colonel's company. Only the golden silk fringe identifies it as a dragoon standard rather than an infantry flag.

D: Lithuania, 1721
Despite the treaty of Nystadt (1721) large elements of the Russian army remained garrisoned in Poland and Lithuania. Breakdowns in the military supply system meant that hardships for the local populations continued, until a system of organised billeting was introduced.

D1, 2: Troopers, Line Dragoon Regiment
These troopers wear the new cut of uniform introduced in 1720, with falling collar and simplified pocket flaps; the pattern would remain in use until 1735. The cartridge box, belt and carbine sling remained unaltered. D1 is pictured holding a Russian-made carbine, secured by its sling.

D3: Trooper, Dragoon Garrison Regiment
Garrison Dragoons retained a uniform based upon the pre-1720 pattern throughout the period. Under his *kaftan* the trooper has a rough grey working coat, worn on its own when on working parties. Garrison units were always less well supplied than Line units, and their armament would often be old weapons discarded by the regular army, in this case a musketoon.

D4: Praporschik (Ensign), Line Dragoon Regiment
Even the most junior officers could embellish their uniforms as they wished, a freedom denied after Peter's death; both gold trim and officer's sashes were used to differentiate between ranks. This young officer wears a wig variant favoured by officers of the period throughout Europe. His German smallsword is based on an original in the Artillery Museum, St. Petersburg.

E: Vyborg, 1710
The Finnish fortress town of Vyborg was besieged by General-Admiral Apraxin and surrendered following a heavy bombardment from the Russian siege train. The Russians' lack of finesse at siege warfare was compensated for by the improving technical abilities of Peter's gunners.

E1: Bombardier, Artillery Regiment
Created to operate mortars in the train of artillery, Bombardiers could also operate as a form of train guard. Their mitre caps closely resembled those of Guard Grenadiers, although otherwise they retained the Artillery Regiment's uniform. The Bombardier is carrying a brass hand mortar; a form of primitive grenade launcher, fired using an artillery halberd as a rest. He wears an overcoat in the colours recorded as issued to the Artillery Regiment.

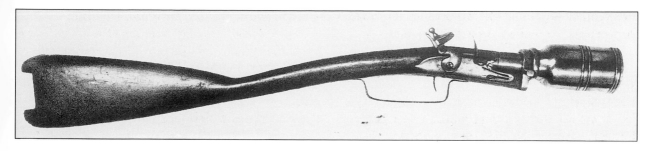

▲ *A Petrine hand mortar. Issued to artillery bombardiers, these seemingly impractical weapons had a bore of 49 mm, and fired a small grenade. They continued to be used after Tsar Peter's reign. (State Museums of the Moscow Kremlin)*

▶ *Bombardier c.1727–30. His cartridge box bears the monogram of Tsar Peter II (Peter the Great's grandson), but the uniform remained unchanged since 1720. He demonstrates the method of firing by resting the hand mortar on a specially issued halberd. (The Hermitage Museum, St. Petersburg)*

E2, 3: Cannoniers, Artillery Regiment

Petrine gunners were recruited from the more intelligent conscripts, and were paid at a higher rate than other soldiers. These men wear the pre-1720 pattern artillery uniform, of an identical cut to that of infantrymen. For close support cannoniers were armed with a musket and cartridge pouch, which would be set aside when manning the artillery piece.

E4: Junior officer, Artillery Regiment

Artillery officers underwent specialist training, often abroad, and were considered to be amongst the most skilled men in the army. The figure is based partly on the portrait (reproduced in MAA 260, p.9) of Sergei Bukhvostov, 'the first Russian soldier', who served as an artillery officer at Vyborg.

F: St. Petersburg, 1724

By 1724, St. Petersburg, founded by Tsar Peter, was becoming an important cosmopolitan city. The Life Regiment of Life Guard Cavalry was established in the city partly as a training school for young officers, but was increasingly relied upon for ceremonial duties in the new capital.

F1: Life Guard cavalry trooper, Life Regiment

This young gentleman wears the uniform particular to the Guard Cavalry, with an embroidered surcoat over his *kaftan*. Troopers of the regiment were ranked as NCOs, and consequently were allowed to

wear gold braid on their cuff turnbacks. This trooper has a Russian-made carbine slung on a bandolier.

F2: Life Guard cavalry major, Life Regiment

The major's rank is denoted by his extensive braiding. Officer's sashes were optional in this regiment. Guard officers achieved their position through merit, but the privileges of rank then allowed them to become involved in court politics and intrigues.

F3: Prince Menshikov

Alexander Menshikov's rise from obscurity to court favourite gave him the opportunity to make himself one of the wealthiest men in Russia. Following a

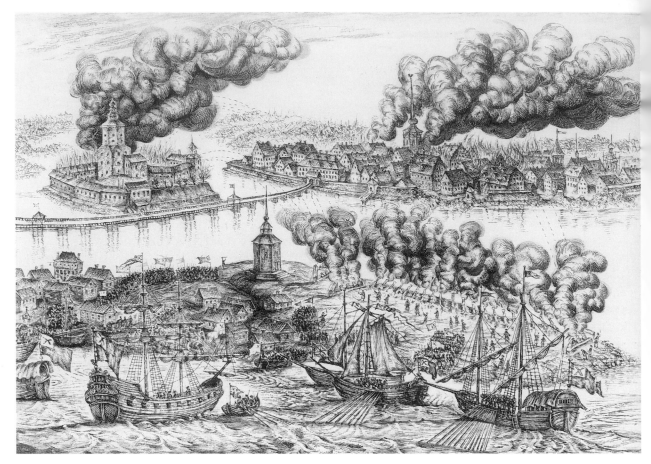

Modern reconstruction of the siege of Vyborg (1710). Apraxin's siege battery is located on the spit in the foreground, facing the vulnerable medieval section of town wall over the harbour. Ink and watercolour by Dillosov, 1991. (Author's collection)

successful military career, his position as 'friend of the Tsar' enabled him to increase his power, but he was exiled for corruption after the death of the Empress Catherine. He wears the order of St. Andrew, a victory medal, and a Polish order awarded after the battle of Kalisz.

G: Stockholm, 1719
During Apraxin's raids on the mainland of Sweden, Cossacks and Kalmuks were landed from the fleet to ravage deep into the Swedish countryside. Cossacks were even reported on the outskirts of Stockholm, creating panic in the city. These raids played a large part in forcing the Swedes to sue for peace.

G1: Don Cossack
This 'kazak' wears the typical long *kaftan*, baggy breeches and high boots of the Don host. He carries a curved sabre and Caucasian rifled musket. No uniform was worn, and items of looted apparel might be pressed into service. He is depicted leading a second pony, used to carry provisions and plunder.

G2: Don Cossack commander
The post of regimental commander was an elected one, although it normally fell to a relatively wealthy landowner. The dress of this officer reflects both wealth and status, and he carries a mace as a badge of rank. The saddle is typical of those produced by Ukrainian craftsmen.

G3: Kalmuk horseman
This Asiatic auxiliary in Russian service wears the embroidered silk tunic, headgear and 'Turkish-style' footwear described by 18th century travellers in Russia. His bow, arrows, quiver and sword are based on examples held in the Russian Museum, St. Petersburg.

H: Flags and standards
H1: Company standard, Goltz's Dragoon Regiment, 1700

This is typical of the company standards used by both Dragoons and noble cavalry regiments at Narva. The cyrillic inscription reads 'By this sign we conquer'. (Source: Petrelli and Legrelius)

H2: Company standard, Moskovski Dragoon Regiment, 1712–25

A 1712-pattern standard, it bears the Muscovite crowned eagle carrying the badge of Moscow. (Source: Viskovatov)

H3: Streltsi standard, late 17th century

Probably a standard of the Novgorod *Streltsi* regiment, it displays the Orthodox cross flanked by the Emperor Constantine and Empress Helena. It was lost to the Swedes at Narva. (Source: Petrelli and Legrelius)

H4: Possible artillery standard, 1700

The Muscovite eagle over a trophy of arms is depicted on the field of the Russian tricolour first introduced by Peter I. This may well be the 'standard of the Train' captured at Narva. The dashed line marks the shape of the damaged original, now in Stockholm. (Source: Petrelli and Legrelius)

H5: Company colour, Guard infantry regiment, 1712–25

Issued to both the Guard infantry regiments (see MAA 260), this flag bears the Cyrillic inscriptions 'The Lord Christ is our Sovereign', with 'By this sign I shall triumph' in the upper canton. (Source: Viskovatov)

H6: Standard, Life Regiment of Life Guard cavalry, 1719–25

Based on the pattern of the guidon of Menshikov's Life Squadron, this cavalry standard bears the cross of St. Andrew surmounted by the Tsarist crown. (Source: Viskovatov)

BIBLIOGRAPHY

This is only a selection of works which cover aspects of the Petrine army or reflect contemporary opinions of it. Unfortunately, little is available in English.

L.G. Beskrovnyi, *Russkaya Armiya i Flot v XVIII Veke* (Moscow 1958)

Poltava. K 250-Letiyu Poltavskogo Srazheniya (Moscow 1959)

P.H. Bruce, *Memoirs of Peter Henry Bruce Esq.* (London 1782)

P. Condray, *Swedish and Russian armies of the Great Northern War* (New York 1990)

C. Duffy, *Russia's Military Way to the West* (London 1981)

P. Englund, *Poltava* (Stockholm 1988, trans. London 1992)

R. Hatton (ed.), *Captain Jeffereye's letters from the Swedish army, 1707–9* (Stockholm 1954)

J.G. Korb, *Diary of an Austrian Secretary of Legation at the Court of Tsar Peter* (London 1863)

V. Klyuchevsky, *Peter the Great* (London 1958)

C. von Manstein, *Memoires sur la Russie*, 3 vols. (Paris 1860)

R.G. Massie, *Peter the Great* (London 1991)

C.F. Masson, *Memoires Secrets sur la Russie* (Paris 1859)

N. Orlov, *Italyanski Pokhod Suvorova v. 1799* (St. Petersburg 1898)

J. Perry, *The state of Russia* (London 1716)

Petrelli & Legrelius, *Narvatrofféer* (Stockholm 1907)

F. von Stein, *Geschichte der Russischen Heeres* (Hanover 1885)

A.V. Viskovatov, *Opisaniye Obmundirovaniya ... Russiskoi Imperatorskoi Armii*, 30 vols. (St. Petersburg 1844–5)

F.C. Weber, *Das Verandere Russland* (Frankfurt 1744)

W. Zweguintzow, *L'Armee Russe*, 2 vols. (Paris 1967)

Notes sur les planches en couleurs

A Le niveau de pugnacité des unités de cavalerie russe traditionnelle n'était pas des plus elevées comme en témoignent leur fuite et leur refus de combattre lors de la bataille de Narva en 1700. A1 A cette époque, la haute noblesse était déjà fortement influencée par l'occident comme en témoignent ces manteaux de cuir chamois. A2 Les Moscovites se considéraient comme l'élite de la cavalerie aristocratique et leur vêtements étaient encore plus influencés par la mode occidentale que ceux des cavaliers provenant de provinces reculées. A3, 4 Ces cavaliers portent l'habit traditionnel, inspiré de celui des *Streltsi* et reconstitué d'après des gravures d'époque. Les armes, ainsi que toutes les autres figurant sur ces planches, sont conformes aux exemplaires exposés dans des musées russes.

B Les dragons constituaient le gros de la cavalerie russe. Ils pouvaient se battre à pied (conformément aux tactiques en vigeur au 17ème siècle) aussi bien qu'à cheval. B1, 2 L'uniforme du modèle 1700–1720 et porté ici avec le chapeau du type 'kartuz'. Comme les cartouchières de dragons n'étaient pas toujours disponible en quantité suffisante, il arrivait qu'on leur substitue le modèle d'infanterie. B3 Les officiers avaient une plus grande liberté dans le choix de leur uniforme. Celui-ci porte un manteau qui date d'avant 1720 par dessus son *kaftan* (veste uniforme). L'écharpe portée en bandoulière indique le grade. B4, 5 La plupart des règiments de dragons portait le tricorne et un *kaftan* d'une couleur chosie par leur colonel. Les dragons étaient équipés d'un mousquet raccourci.

C La charge des dragons russes à Poltava fut une influence déterminante sur le cours de la bataille. C1 Après avoir tiré une salve de mousquet ou de carabine (arme de cavalerie plus courte) à une distance de 25–35 mètres, les dragons s'élançaient l'arme au clair ou pistolet au poing. La plupart des pistolets provenaient de Hollande. C2 L'uniforme était presqu'identique à celui des grenadiers, quoiqu'il soit impossible à un cavalier sur sa monture de lancer des grenades. Les grenadiers de Von der Ropp avaient des uniformes rouges, et ceux de Roshnov des verts. C3 Les simples tambours étaient utilisés pour battre la charge lors des combats à pied, quoique les dragons aient aussi eu des timbales et des trompettes. C4 Les étandards des dragons étaient quasiment identiques aux drapeaux de l'infanterie, sauf pour la frange de soie dorée.

D1, 2 Le nouvel uniforme de 1721 avait un col chevalière et des poches d'un modèle plus simple. A noter la carabine de fabrication russe, dont la sangle coulisse grâce à des mousquetons le long d'une tringle en métal fixée sur le côté de l'arme. D3 Les troupes de garnison avaient gardé l'uniforme d'avant 1720. Leur armement aussi était obsolète. Sous son *kaftan* l'homme porte le bourgeron de toile grossière utilisé pour les corvées. D4 Les écharpes et la passementerie de canetille dorées étaient les signes distinctifs des officiers. La forme de ces attributs ne seront définies qu'après la mort de Pierre le Grand.

E1 Les servant d'obusiers avaient aussi pour fonction de garder le pièces d'artillerie. Leur uniforme s'apparentait à celui des grenadiers de la garde. L'obusier portatif était tirée en le repoussant sur une halebarde. E2, 3 L'uniforme d'avant 1720. Les servant des pièces d'artillerie laissaient de côté mousquet et giberne quand ils s'affèraient autour de leur pièce. E4 Illustration inspirée d'un portrait de Sergei Bukhvostov qui servit en tant qu'officier d'artillerie à Vyborg.

F Le Tsar Pierre n'avait que peu de cavalerie ordinaire car il préfère les dragons. Le Régiment de Cavalerie de la Garde n'a été créé qu'en 1722 et fut cantonné à St Petersbourg où il servait aussi comme école d'officiers. F1 Un surtout brodé porté sur le kaftan de dragon faisait le signe le plus distinctif de l'uniforme de la cavalerie de la garde. La passementerie était en canetille et tous les cavaliers de ce régiment d'élite avaient le grade de sous-officier. F2 Une profusion de galons dorés indique le grade de major. Dans cette unité, le port de l'écharpe était facultatif. F3 D'origine modeste, cet officier a gravi tous les échelons pour devenir le favori de la cour du roi Pierre. Après de brillants services dans l'armée, il fut éxilé pour corruption.

G En 1719, la Suède fut mise à sac par des cosaques qui y avaient été transportés par la marine russe. G1 Ils n'avaient pas d'uniforme particulier et leur tenue pouvait être agrémentée d'effets volés au cours de leurs rapines. Souvent, un second poney transportait les provisions et le butin. G2 En règle générale, les chefs cosaques étaient choisis parmi les gros propriétaires terriens comme l'indique leur habillement plus recherché. La masse d'armes était une marque de grade. G3 Un petit nombre d'auxiliaires asiatiques servait dans les rangs russes. La plupart d'entre eux étaient encore armés d'arcs et de flèches.

H1 Modèle caractéristique utilisé par les dragons jusqu'à la bataille de Narva en 1700. H2 Guidon d'une compagnie de dragon, modèle 1712, avec l'aigle moscovite et l'emblème de la ville. H3 Drapeau qui aurait pu appartenir au régiment de *Streltsi* de Novgorod, décoré d'une croix orthodoxe et d'une représentation de l'empereur Constantine et de l'impératrice Hélène. H4 Capturé à la bataille de Narva, ce drapeau est peut-être celui du train d'artillerie. Le drapeau tricolore a été introduit par le tsar Pierre. H5 Distribué aux deux régiments d'infanterie de la garde. H6 Ce modèle est basé sur le guidon de l'escadron de garde personele Menshikov qui, dès 1722, faisait partie du régiment de cavalerie de la garde.

Farbtafeln

A Die traditionelle Kavallerie 'russischen Stils' war von sehr schlechter Qualität und floh 1700 bei der Schlacht von Narwa ohne zu kämpfen. A1 Einige Adlige höheren Ranges hatten sich inzwischen westliche Kleidungsmerkmale, wie etwa 'Ledermäntel' zu eigen gemacht. A2 Die Moskowiter sahen sich als die Elite der adligen Kavallerie; ihre Uniform war unter Umständen etwas mehr von westlichen Einflüssen geprägt, als das in den entlegenen Provinzen der Fall war. A3, A4 Dieser Provinzkavallerist trägt die traditionelle Uniform, die auf der von *Streltsi* getragenen beruht und zeitgenössischen westlichen Stichen nachempfunden wurde. Seine Waffen—wie alle auf diesen Tafeln abgebildeten—sind erhaltenen Exemplaren in russischen Museen nachgebildet.

B Die Dragoner stellten den Großteil der russischen Kavallerie. Sie kämpften noch abgesessen (nach Art des 17. Jahrhunderts) als auch zu Pferde. B1, B2 Die Uniform Modell 1700–1720 wird hier mit einer *Kartuz*-Mütze getragen. Die kleinere Patronentasche für Dragoner war oft nicht lieferbar, und man gab stattdessen das Infanteriemodell aus. B3 Offiziere hatten bei der Wahl ihrer Uniform mehr Spielraum; dieser Offizier trägt einen Offiziersmantel des Modells, das vor 1720 gebräuchlich war, über seinem *Kaftan* (Uniformjacke), und seine Schärpe gibt den Offiziersrang an. B4, B5 Die meisten Dragonerregimente trugen den Dreispitz und den Uniform-*Kaftan* in einer Farbe, die von ihrem Oberst gewählt wurde. Zu Anfang waren die Dragoner mit verkürzten Musketen ausgerüstet.

C Die berittene Attacke der russischen Dragoner bei Poltawa spielte in dieser Schlacht eine entscheidende Rolle. C1 Nachdem sie Musketen oder Karabiner in einer Schußweite von 25–35 Metern abgefeuert hatten, gingen die Dragoner mit gezogenen Pistolen beziehungsweise Säbeln zum Angriff über. Bei den meisten dieser Pistolen handelte es sich um holländische Importartikel. Die Mündung des umgehängten Karabiners steckte in einem 'Schuh', der mit einem Gurt am Sattel befestigt war. C2 Die Uniform ist mit der der Infanterie-Grenadiere fast identisch, obgleich Gewehrgranaten zu Pferde nicht eingesetzt werden konnten. Von der Ropp-Grenadiere trugen rote Uniformen, Roschnow-Grenadiere grüne. C3 Für den Kampf zu Fuß wurden herkömmliche Trommeln ausgegeben, obwohl Dragoner außerdem Kesselpauker und Trompeter hatten.

D1, D2 1721 wurde eine neue Dragoneruniform mit Umlegkragen und vereinfachten Taschen herausgegeben; die Lederausrüstung blieb unverändert. Dieses Figur trägt einen Karabiner russischer Fertigung an einem Schultergurt, der an einem Riegel an der Seite des Karabiners befestigt ist. D3 Garnisonseinheiten behielten die Uniformen des Modells vor 1720 sowie veraltete Schußwaffen bei. Unter seinem *Kaftan* trägt er eine grobe Arbeitsjacke, die lediglich für den Arbeitsdienst getragen wurde. D4 Schärpen und goldfarbene Uniformbesätze kennzeichneten Offiziere, die genaue Anordnung der Goldbesätze wurde erst nach dem Tod des Zaren Peter geregelt.

E1 Bombardiere, die Mörser bedienten, fungierten gleichzeitig als Wachen für die Artillerie; die Uniformen glichen denen der Gardegrenadiere. Man beachte den 'Hand-Mörser'—ein Granatwerfer, der abgefeuert wurde, indem man ihn auf der Hellebarde abstützte. E2, E3 Uniform aus den Jahren vor 1720; die Muskete und Tasche wurden zur Geschützbedienung beiseite gelegt. E4 Gründet sich teilweise auf ein Porträt von Sergej Bukhwostow, der in Vyborg als Artillerieoffizier diente.

F Zar Peter beschäftigte sehr wenige reguläre Kavalleristen. Das Leibregiment der Gardekavallerie wurde erst 1722 gegründet und hatte in St. Petersburg als Offiziersschule seinen ständigen Standort. F1 Ein bestickter Überzug, der über dem normalen Dragoner-*Kaftan* getragen wurde, war das Hauptmerkmal der Uniform der Gardekavallerie. Reiter dieses Eliteregiments hatten Unteroffiziersrang und trugen Tressenbesatz. F2 Umfassende Goldtressen kennzeichnen den Rang des Majors; in dieser Einheit wurden Offiziersschärpen freiwillig getragen. F3 Dieser Offizier wurde als Günstling am Hof des Zaren Peter bekannt; er war ein erfolgreicher Soldat, wurde jedoch später wegen Bestechlichkeit verbannt.

G 1719 wurden Kosaken der russischen Flotte in Schweden an Land gebracht und verwüsteten dort die Landschaft. G1 Sie trugen keine Uniform, sondern herkömmliche Bekleidung, die vielleicht durch Beutestücke ergänzt wurde. Man führte ein Zweitpferd mit, das Vorräte und Plündergut trug. G2 Die Anführer der Kosaken wurden für gewöhnlich aus den Kreisen wohlhabender Landbesitzer gewählt, was sich in ihrer guten Aufmachung niederschlug; der Streitkolben war ein Zeichen des Rangs. G3 Außerdem wurden gelegentlich asiatische Hilfstruppen eingesetzt, die oft noch Pfeil und Bogen benutzten.

H1 Typische Kompanie-Standarte, wie sie von den Dragonern bis zur Schlacht von Narwa 1700 benutzt wurde. H2 Kompanie-Standarte der Dragoner des 1712er Modells, die bei diesem Regiment den Moskowiter-Adler und das Abzeichen der Stadt trägt. H3 Wahrscheinlich die Flagge des *Streltsi*-Regiments von Nowgorod, auf der das orthodoxe Kreuz vom Kaiser Konstantin und der Kaiserin Helena flankiert wird. H4 Dies ist eventuell die Flagge des Artilleriezuges, der in Narwa gefangengenommen wurde. Zar Peter fürte als Erster die russische Trikolore ein. H5 Wurde an beide Garde-Infanterieregimenter ausgegeben. H6 Muster, das auf der Standarte der Menschikow-Leibschwadron beruht, die 1722 Teil des Leibregiments der Gardekavallerie darstellte.